AMERICA, AERONWY, AND ME
Dylan Thomas Tribute Tour

ALSO BY PETER THABIT JONES

Poetry

Tacky Brow (Outposts Publications, UK, 1974)
The Apprenticeship (Cwm Nedd Press, UK, 1977)
Clocks Tick Differently (Celtion Poetry Series, UK, 1980)
Visitors (Poetry Wales Press, UK, 1986)
The Cold Cold Corner (Dark Lane Poetry, UK, 1995)
Ballad of Kilvey Hill (Swansea Bay Publishers/Eastside Poetry, UK, 1999)
The Lizard Catchers (Cross-Cultural Communications, USA, 2006 /reprinted 2007 & 2008)
POET TO POET #1: Bridging the Waters: Swansea to Sag Harbor, with American poet Vince Clemente (Cross-Cultural Communications, USA, and The Seventh Quarry Press, UK, 2008)
Whispers of the Soul, with American poet Vince Clemente (a bilingual collection: English/Romanian). Translated by Dr. Olimpia Iacob (Editura Fundatiei Poezia Iasi, Romania, 2008)
Poems from a Cabin on Big Sur (Cross-Cultural Communications, USA, 2011)
Where the Butterflies Go/Songs for a Dark Bird (Two bilingual collections of poems in one book. Romania's Aura Cristi's *Where the Butterflies Go*/Peter's *Songs for a Dark Bird*. Translated by Dr. Olimpia Iacob and Jim Kacian (Timpul Publishing, Romania, 2014)
Selected Poems (bilingual collection: English/Romanian). Translated by Dr. Monica Manolachi of the University of Bucharest. (Bibliotecha Universalis/Collectiile Revistei 'Orizont Literar Contemporan', Romania, 2016)

Prose

Dylan Thomas Walking Tour of Greenwich Village, New York, with Aeronwy Thomas (for the Wales International Centre, New York/Welsh Assembly Government, 2008, (PDF www.walesworldnation.com)
PODCAST: www.dylanthomaswalkingtourmp3.com
Dylan Thomas Walking Tour of Greenwich Village, New York tourist pocket book, with Aeronwy Thomas (Cross-Cultural Communications, USA, and The Seventh Quarry Press, UK, 2014)
Dylan Thomas Walking Tour of Greenwich Village, New York smartphone app, with Aeronwy Thomas (DT100/Dylan Thomas Centenary, Welsh Government, Literature Wales, and The British Council, 2014)

Drama

The Boy and the Lion's Head/A Verse Drama (bilingual: English/Romanian). Translated by Dr. Olimpia Iacob (Citadela Publishing, Romania, 2009)
The Fire in the Wood/A Prose and Verse Drama, (Cross-Cultural Communications, USA, and The Seventh Quarry Press, UK, 2017)
The Boy and the Lion's Head/A Verse Drama (New Feral Press, USA, 2017)

DVDs

Walking with Dylan Thomas/documentary film based on the *Dylan Thomas Walking Tour of Greenwich Village* (Cross-Cultural Communications, USA, and The Seventh Quarry Press, UK, 2010)
The Poet, the Hunchback, and the Boy/drama (Dylan Thomas Theatre, Holly Tree Productions, and The Seventh Quarry Press, 2014)

Peter Thabit Jones

AMERICA, AERONWY, AND ME
Dylan Thomas Tribute Tour

(includes contributions from some
of those who hosted us on the tour)

Cross-Cultural Communications
New York, USA

The Seventh Quarry Press,
Swansea, Wales, UK
2019

Copyright © 2019 by Peter Thabit Jones
Copyright © 2019 Foreword by Stanley H. Barkan
Copyright © 2019 Texts by Laura Boss, Catrin Brace, Kristine Doll,
John Dotson, Maria Mazziotti Mazziotti Gillan, Paul M. Levitt,
Beverly Matherne, Carol Menkiti, Tino Villanueva
Copyright © 2008 Photos by Peter Thabit Jones
Copyright © 2019 Photos of Hosts by Laura Boss, Catrin Brace, Kristine Doll,
John Dotson, Pavel Grushko, Peter Thabit Jones, Paul M. Levitt,
Beverly Matherne, Bill Wolak
Copyright © 2019 Photo by Martin Holroyd
Copyright © 2017 Photo by Robin V. Robinson
Copyright © 2019 Portrait by Svetlana Deric Jannace
Copyright © 2019 Supplement Poems by Stanley H. Barkan, Peter Thabit Jones,
and Aeronwy Thomas (with the permission of Trefor Ellis)
Copyright © 2019 Front and back covers by Tamara Dellutri

All rights reserved under International Copyright Conventions. Except for brief passages quoted in a newspaper, magazine, or television or Internet review, no part of this book may be reproduced in any form or by any means electronic or mechanical, including photocopying and recording or by any information storage and retrieval system, without permission in writing from the publishers or the authors.

Cross-Cultural Communications
239 Wynsum Avenue
Merrick, New York 11566-4725 USA
Tel: (516) 868-5635 / Fax: (516) 379-1901
cccpoetry@aol.com
www.cross-culturalcommunications.com

The Seventh Quarry Press
8 Cherry Crescent
Swansea SA4 9FG Wales, UK
Tel: (UK) 07964039928
info@peterthabitjones.com
www.peterthabitjones.com

Library of Congress Control Number: 2018952169
ISBN 978-0-89304-671-2
Front and back covers by Tamara Dellutri

First Edition
Printed in Wales by Dinefwr Print & Design, Llandybie, Carmarthenshire, Wales, UK

ACKNOWLEDGMENTS

To Stanley H. Barkan, poet and our American publisher, for his incredible two years diligent work on organising the tour for Aeronwy and me and to him and Bebe Barkan, his artist wife, for hosting and entertaining us at Casa Barkan and for driving us to various events and leisure places.

To emeritus professor, poet and critic Vince Clemente for his consultation with Stanley during the two years of organising everything.

To those of our hosts throughout the tour, who organised our events and lodgings in their localities and for their driving us to events and leisure places.

To Stanley H. Barkan for his Foreword to this book.

To some of our hosts and organisers who have contributed to this book.

To Trefor Ellis, husband of Aeronwy Thomas, for endorsing this book and allowing the use of work by Aeronwy Thomas.

To Hannah Ellis, daughter of Trefor and Aeronwy, for endorsing this book.

To Martin Holroyd, Aeronwy's British publisher, who took the photo of us at the Dylan Thomas Centre, which was used as the official tour photo.

To Carolyn Mary Kleefeld, American poet and artist, for my eighth and ninth writer-in residence opportunities in California in the summers of 2017 and 2018, when I worked on parts of this book.

IN MEMORY OF AERONWY THOMAS (1943–2009)

FOR STANLEY H. BARKAN AND VINCE CLEMENTE

CONTENTS

Foreword 13

Introduction 19

The Dylan Thomas Tribute Tour of America 23

Postscript 126

Bios of the Tour hosts who contributed to this book 131

Poems Supplement 134

Bio of Stanley H. Barkan 145

Bio of Aeronwy Thomas 148

About the Author 150

FOREWORD

HOW IT ALL STARTED

To quote Dylan Thomas, to begin at the beginning . . .

Our mutual long-term poet friend, Vince Clemente, sent Peter some of my books–those in which my original poetry was published, and others I had published as a small press publisher. Not long afterward, Peter wrote inviting me to be the first featured poet at the Dylan Thomas Centre in Swansea, Wales, as part of The Seventh Quarry Press series of events. Well, I was overwhelmed. I felt that I had died and gone to Heaven, as a poet, since whenever I felt I couldn't write anymore, I would read Dylan and could again.

And there was another enhancing reason for this feeling. My daughter, Mia, as a little girl was having severe pains in her belly. After several false diagnoses, I decided to take the advice of my Romanian friend, Eva Feiler, to go see a Romanian-born, Dr. Fingerhut, in New York, who was a responsible for the invention of the artificial kidney machine. My wife, Bebe, initially demurred, as Dr. Fingergut, who was associated with the Columbia-Presbyterian (now New York-Presbyterian) hospital in New York, was a good hour or more ride from Merrick. She thought it would be more convenient to have Mia in a local, nearby hospital. But I wanted my daughter to have the best possible doctor's diagnosis. Dr. Fingerhut said he wasn't sure, but arranged for x-rays and other analysis at Columbia-Presbyterian.

We took Mia there, she in pain, "My belly hurts, Daddy!" all the way in. I stayed in the children's ward, waiting the prognosis. As I was very anxious, I slipped into the radiology ward and heard two doctors saying, "They're all reversed!" Thus, I discovered that Mia had *situs inversus*–all of her organs are reversed, a rare condition, only 300 other cases known in the world at that time. Also, she had four kidneys, two of which had become nephritic. She ultimately had three operations by a Dr. Uson, who had a new procedure he was practicing all over the world. I never left Mia to be alone in the hospital. They allowed me to sleep over. I always had my New Directions copy of Dylan's *Collected Poems*, which I read and re-read, and was sustained by Dylan's wisdom and richness of imagery. Thus, Peter's invitation was a very special gift.

Bebe and I took the first plane out in 2006. We struggled with bags full of books in Victoria Station, as there was no elevator. We took the train to Cardiff, where Peter picked us up and drove us to Swansea, where we stayed in a hotel where one of his son's worked, thus, permitting us a good discount.

We walked around Swansea, visited Dylan's birthplace, saw his statue, and eventually had dinner together in Mumbles. The car was left in a car-park about 100 yards from the restaurant. The weather was clear when we arrived, but turned to cold and wet and windy when we left. I had forgotten to take my trusty scarf. I pictured it still hanging on a hook in the foyer of my house in Merrick. Well, I developed a cold and a very sore throat. What to do the next day when the audience would be coming to hear me read?

The day of the reading it was quite stormy. Still a good crowd of more than 100 came, including Peter's wife and children and Aeronwy, daughter of Dylan, with Martin Holroyd, her British publisher, and, even–an incredible surprise–Anne, the Scottish (bigamy) wife of my Sicilian friend, Nat Scammacca, and the daughter, Lee Scammacca. Well, I was heartened by such a crowd and that some, like Aeronwy and Martin who came all the way from England, and Ann & Lee who had come from Scotland–both some 300 kilometres each.

Despite my sore throat and debilitating cold, I read for about an hour and a half, and answered many questions till I felt I could go on no longer. Then suggested that the audience look at the books I'd brought. I had the best sale ever, except for Sicilian audiences, but, in this case, my work had little to do with Wales, except for the influence of Dylan. It was during and after my signing the books that I chatted with Aeronwy and Martin, and Ann and Lee. I spent as much time with all four as I could then begged off to get some rest but said that I hoped to see them in the morning.

In the morning, Aeronwy, Martin, and Peter came to the breakfast we shared. Then I got to see some of Aeronwy's poetry in the books Martin had published, and her manuscript, which Peter had handed to me on Bebe's and my arrival at the hotel. Eureka! Impressed by how nice Aeronwy was and talented as well, since I always try for any kindness I receive, in accordance with Japanese *gimu* or *gisu* practice, to repay threefold, my thoughts about arranging a nation-wide tour of America for her and Peter started to cook.

I knew I'd have to rely on the many CCC authors who are also professors to provide venues with significant fees to cover costs and to make it worthwhile for Aeronwy and Peter. Thus, the first two items which were the *sine qua non* of the possibility of the tour: 1. Money to pay their airfare from UK to US and 2. One high-paying fee at a significant venue. It was Sultan Catto, world-famous physicist, who is also a poet, offered $2,000 to solve the first issue. Then it was Maria Mazziotti Gillan, poet-Director of the Poetry Center at Passaic County Community College, in Paterson, New Jersey, who offered another $2,000 for both to be featured in her Distinguished Poets Series. With these two issues, if you will, in my pocket, I knew I had a foundation for the tour.

Building on this foundation of the airline cost covered and a major reading at Passaic County Community College, I was ready to cast a wide net to the Cross-Cultural Communications family. This broke down into the following: 1. Local and East Coast events; 2. Travel Arrangements to Midwest and Far West; 3. Events in the Midwest and Far West; 4. Return to New York, for final events; 5. Follow up. Ultimately, the tour was set for April 1–May 5, with Aeronwy's choir-singer husband, Trefor Ellis joining the East Coast part of the tour, April 7–18. Despite some disappointing lack of response from the 92nd Street Y, where Dylan made his debut in America in 1950 (not even a call back) and Long Island and New York colleges, the net resulted in some 28 venues across the country, with an international component as well, featuring translations of Dylan's poetry into 17 different languages.

Casa Barkan was the base for Aeronwy, Peter, and Trefor: Peter stayed in what was our daughter Mia's room, while Aeronwy and Trefor stayed in what was our son Scotte's room, now, because of all the decorations from Asia, called the "Asia Room." Locally, the start was a welcome party at Casa Barkan, to which our Barkan family and friends and Cross-Cultural Communications nearby authors came to welcome Aeronwy and Peter, and the first-ever nation-wide Dylan Thomas Tribute Tour was off to the poetry races.

Some of the more significant venues included (on Long Island) the Walt Whitman Birthplace in Huntington, The Stevenson Academy of Fine Arts in Oyster Bay, (in NYC) the Wales International Centre in the Chrysler Building, The CUNY Graduate Center, The National Arts Club, the White Horse Tavern, (in New Jersey) Hamilton House and Passaic County Community College in Paterson, (in Massachusetts) the Salem State University, Wellesley College in Wellesley, The Grolier Poetry Book Shop, The John Adams House, the Woodberry Room at the Houghton Library at Harvard University in Cambridge, (in Michigan) Women's Federated Clubhouse, Northern Michigan University in Marquette, (in Illinois) Knox College in Galesburg, the Chicago Poetry Society, the Green Mill Jazz Club, Vitalist Theatre Company in Chicago, (in Iowa) the Shambaugh House at the Iowa International Writing Workshop, the University of Iowa, (in Colorado) the University of Colorado at Boulder, the Canyon Theater, (in California) the Robin Jeffers Tor House, and the Monterey Peninsula College. Many of the hosts welcomed Aeronwy and Trefor and Peter in their homes. There were also numerous interviews on radio and in local newspapers and magazines. Most of the East Coast programs, too, were videotaped for posterity.

I'm grateful to all who, in the words of Aeronwy, helped "as a byproduct," to revitalize interest in Dylan Thomas. Their arrangement efforts and generosity was truly a tribute to the legacy of Dylan Thomas. Special thanks, too, must be accorded to those who, in addition to providing a public venue, opened their homes to welcome Aeronwy and Trefor and Peter: Bebe Barkan, Sultan and Neslihan Catto, Kristine Doll, Beverly Matherne, Tammy Nuzzo-Morgan, Paul and Nancy Levitt, Ken and Jane Schwartz. Special thanks are also due to the translators, some of whom traveled a great distance to be physically present at the Mid-Manhattan Library: Kristine Doll (Massachusetts), Silvia Kofler (Missouri), Kyung-nyun Kim "Kay" Richards (California).

Special mention is also due to those who provided and continue to do so, return trips for Peter to East Meadow (Jude Schanzer), Salem (Kristine Doll and Peter H. Fulton), Cambridge (Ifeanyi A. Menkiti), Colorado (Paul M. Levitt), and New York (Sultan Catto)–most especially for the Dylan Thomas Walking Tour of Greenwich Village (Catrin Brace), and the return of Peter to Big Sur as Poet-in-Residence for the last nine years, provided by Carolyn Mary Kleefeld with Patricia Holt, resulting from John Dotson's introduction. Something must also be said about the CCC family of authors bringing students to Dylan Thomas's Wales (i.e., Robin Metz from Knox College), and all who traveled there, too, to participate in the International Poetry Festival in Honor of Dylan Thomas.

I'm also saddened by the early demise, just a year later, of Aeronwy, who suffered from a blood disease, which she kept very privately to herself; thus, she was not able to participate in the follow-up invitations. I miss her morning cups of tea, her saying, "When it comes to food, go to Stanley," and her fervent dedication to her father's legacy. In one event, when she read her poem, "Sorry," about Bob Dylan, the singer, who claimed that "he did more for DT than DT ever did for him," Aeronwy took him to task, asserting, "That's my dad you're talking about!"

Her voice and presence still resound in Casa Barkan.

But, most of all, I'm grateful to Vince Clemente, without whose good offices, Peter and I would never have met; to Aeronwy and Peter for taking on this enormous task and fulfilling it so professionally;

also to Trefor Ellis for his enormous contribution as a tenor singer of Welsh songs, and actor in the part of Reverend Eli Jenkins from Dylan's *Under Milk Wood.* Finally, I'm humbled and grateful for the privilege and honor of my role as organizer in perhaps reawakening interest in the legacy of Dylan Thomas with this first-ever nationwide tribute tour.

Diolch yn fawr!
Stanley H. Barkan

INTRODUCTION

I first heard the name Dylan Thomas when I was a new pupil in Danygraig Boys Comprehensive School in Port Tennant, Swansea. I was almost eleven and a half years old when Mr. James, our English Literature teacher, ignited a desire in me to be a poet. He introduced us to the poem *The Kingfisher* by Welsh poet W. H. Davies, and the opening line "It was the rainbow gave thee birth" blew me away. The word *rainbow* lit up in my mind. I could not believe that one carefully chosen word could convey so much. I had once seen a kingfisher when I was playing with friends down by Port Tennant Canal.

He then read *The Hunchback in the Park* by Dylan Thomas, but oddly did not say the poet was born in Swansea, indeed the west side of the town: the posh side to those of us living on the "ugly" side of Dylan's "ugly, lovely town". I don't think we had a hunchback in our area. Certainly I had never seen one. I could, though, and I did feel sympathy for the mocked and lonely "solitary mister" and I loved such lines as "While the boys among the willows/Made the tigers jump out of their eyes" and "the wild boys innocent as strawberries". I also really did think, though I could not understand why, that he lived in a "kennel in the dark".

Aged about thirteen, and determined to be a poet, I joined Swansea Central Library and I immediately scanned its Poetry section, to find books by Dylan Thomas. I also discovered a treasure-chest of other poets, such as Gerard Manley Hopkins, Thomas Hardy, Emily Dickinson, W. B. Yeats, Edward Thomas, W. H. Auden, Vernon Watkins, Sylvia Plath, and Ted Hughes. I became a regular and very keen customer at the library. Later on, I discovered that Dylan Thomas also made use of the library when he was alive and living in Swansea.

At the same time, I worked as a newspaper boy after school, to earn pocket money, and I started to collect J. M. Dent's Aldine Paperback editions of the works of Dylan Thomas. I still have them. Over the years, I began to buy and read all the books, available at the time, by and about Dylan Thomas; and I built up an impressive personal library of Thomas-related books. I so admired his total commitment to the craft of poetry, the solitary sacred act, as focused as prayer, in front of a blank sheet of paper, and his devotion to a vocation that demands the poet's full attention and will accept no half measures.

At the age of forty-two years, I became a tutor at the Department of Adult Continuing Education, Swansea University, where I taught English Literature, Children's Literature, and Creative Writing on the part-time degree programme for twenty-two years, from 1993 to my early retirement in 2015. Among the courses I taught, was one titled *Poets and Poetry*, which included the works of Dylan Thomas, and a full course on him titled *Singing Light: the Poetry and Prose of Dylan Thomas*.

As that young boy, indeed Dylan fan, I never ever thought I would one day get on a plane at Heathrow Airport and later find myself in America with his daughter, ready to embark on the 2008 Dylan Thomas Tribute Tour, in events stretching from New York to California, To be commissioned at the end of the tour by Catrin Brace of the Welsh Assembly Government in New York, to write the first-ever *Dylan Thomas Walking Tour of Greenwich Village*, was another unexpected blessing.

Aeronwy had a small bird-like quality when standing in front of one, gentle, dignified, and vulnerable. Yet, like the beautiful robin bird, she suggested an inner strength that could survive a "bad winter". During our tour, organised by Stanley H. Barkan, poet and publisher at Cross-Cultural Communications, in consultation with Vince Clemente, emeritus professor, poet and critic, a hectic schedule of demanding weeks of travelling, performing and adjusting ourselves to different living conditions in the various American states, we never had a cross word between us. I remember when at JFK Airport in New York, for our flight to Michigan, I thought I had lost my boarding ticket and we hurriedly retraced our footsteps to the cafeteria area where we had earlier had our cartons of hot tea, only for me to find the ticket in my back pocket of my trousers, and she quietly said, "Not to worry".

In Chicago, where Knox College professor and poet Robin Metz and his professor wife, Liz, hosted us, I realized I needed to buy some extra socks, and Aeronwy traipsed with me through a supermarket. She was as courteous to workers there as she was when introduced to the academic dignitaries we met. Like her famous father, who liked to drink with non-literary people in the Browns Hotel in Laugharne and in the White Horse Tavern in New York, she was not fooled by the social class structure and she approached and responded to all people in the same good-mannered way.

Before the start of each event, she would pass me one of her sweets. "We need a boost," she would say. "You must read your poem *Stones*, they like it," she would tell me. I would ask her to read her beautiful poem *Daughter* and *And death shall have no dominion*, one of her father's early poems, as I loved her readings of both poems, though she brought her own magic to anything she read. With regard to the latter poem, she would reply, "If I have the breath for it." She sometimes finished performances with the poem and the audiences were mesmerised by her spellbinding reading of it.

She signed my copy of her book, *Burning Bridges*, published by Cross-Cultural Communications especially for the tour and for which I wrote the Introduction, "to my comrade". I certainly felt like her comrade during our travelling from New York to California and our various diversions to other states. We looked after each other, like two orphans adopted into the Cross-Cultural Communications "family" of authors. When we were stopping in the hotel in Chicago, she even did my washing in a communal washing machine, one of several there, as I did not know how to use one.

We took to our roles as visiting poets in a very professional manner. A recurring joke between us was we were looking for the best cup of tea in America. We eventually found it in the small and cosy fairytale-like building of the Tuck Box restaurant in Dolores Street, Carmel-By-The-Sea, California, where we were being hosted by American writer and sculptor John Dotson.

It was such a joy when Trefor Ellis, Aeronwy's husband, joined us for two weeks during the tour. We became a performing trio, with Trefor's strong and very engaging singing voice becoming an important and integral addition to our duo's usual programme.

I hope this memento book, published to celebrate the tenth anniversary of the tour, gives the reader some idea of what Aeronwy and I experienced, thanks to Stanley H. Barkan's meticulous and dedicated two years of planning, in consultation with Vince Clemente, and the generously kind and so welcoming hosts and hostesses who helped fulfill Stanley's dream of a 2008 Dylan Thomas Tribute Tour of America featuring Aeronwy and me.

Peter Thabit Jones, 2018

Peter and Aeronwy outside the Dylan Thomas Birthplace, Swansea, before the 2008 Dylan Thomas Tribute Tour.
© 2008 Peter Thabit Jones

THE DYLAN THOMAS TRIBUTE TOUR OF AMERICA, 2008

Aeronwy, Peter, and Stan in the White Horse Tavern, New York.
© 2008 Peter Thabit Jones

It was originally hoped that the tour would coincide with the release of a movie about the Thomases, *The Edge of Love* (aka *The Best Time of Our Lives*, working title), starring Sienna Miller, playing Caitlin MacNamara, Dylan's wife, and Keira Knightly, Vera Phillips, friend of the Thomases, and Mathew Rhys, Dylan Thomas. Director: John Maybury. Producer: Rebekah Gilbertson. Writer Sharman Macdonald (Keira's mother). It was, in fact, released on June 20th, 2008.

The tour featured Aeronwy, answering questions about her father and reading his poems and original poems of her own, principally from her new book, *Burning Bridges*, and me, poet/editor of the Swansea-based poetry magazine, *The Seventh Quarry*, reading my own work, principally from *The Lizard Catchers*, and lecturing on Dylan Thomas, with a focus on the dedicated craftsmanship and obsessive sound-texturing in Dylan's poems and his use of Welsh devices (cyghanedd) in English. We also performed excerpts from her father's famous "A Play for Voices", *Under Milk Wood*.

The sponsors of the tour were Stanley H. Barkan, poet and publisher of Cross-Cultural Communications, in consultation with New York emeritus professor, poet and critic, Vince Clemente.

Peter, Aeronwy, and Trefor outside Casa Barkan, Merrick, Long Island, home of Stanley and Bebe Barkan and the base for the 2008 tour.
© 2008 Peter Thabit Jones

THE NIGHT BEFORE AND OUR ARRIVAL IN NEW YORK

On March 31, 2008, the night before our flight to America, I stayed at Aeronwy's and Trefor's home in Surrey in England. I had travelled from Swansea to London and Trefor picked me up at the bus station. Trefor, who called his wife Aeron, was always good company, warm and welcoming. During the drive to their home and in between chatting with Trefor, I tried to gather my thoughts about what was unfolding. The next day I would be flying to America with the daughter of Dylan Thomas. It seemed somewhat unreal, despite my packed bags and the months of emails and occasional phone calls from Stanley in New York, as he revised and perfected the busy schedule for Aeronwy and me.

I had spent sometime with Aeronwy and Trefor when they had come to Swansea and stopped in an apartment at Swansea Marina for a week or so. We had discussed our schedule and aspects of what poems of our own and works by Dylan Thomas we would offer to American audiences. The three of us did a read-through of some sections from *Under Milk Wood* in the small theatre in the Dylan Thomas Centre in Swansea. I opened as First Voice, Aeronwy and I did Mr. and Mrs. Pugh, Aeronwy did a brilliant Polly Garter, I did some of the Reverend Eli Jenkins, and Trefor sang a beautiful and touching version of Eli Jenkins' Prayer. I recall that the three of us were very pleased with our rehearsals.

When in America, I planned to read from my first American book, *The Lizard Catchers*, published by Cross-Cultural Communications in 2006, and poems from several of my books published in the UK. Aeronwy planned to read from her first American book, *Burning Bridges*, published by Cross-Cultural Communications to coincide with the tour, and from books published by her UK publisher and our mutual friend, Martin Holroyd of Poetry Monthly Press, which was based in Nottinghamshire in England, until his retirement from publishing. It was Martin who took the official tour photo of Aeronwy and me when the three of us were at the Dylan Thomas Centre again, specifically to have a photo taken for Stan to use in the publicity for the tour.

Upon our arrival at their home, Aeronwy greeted Trefor and me and I placed my bags in a convenient spot. After a refreshing cup of tea, Aeronwy showed me her study, which overlooked their back garden. The room was where she steered many of the aspects of her iconic father's legacy as his living "ambassador". Anyone who witnessed the work that she did for the ever-growing Dylan Thomas "industry" could not but admire her professionalism, diligence and focus. It was also the room where she produced her poems and her prose-pieces and I felt honoured to have been shown it. Later on, I was introduced to Huw Dylan, their son, who came down from his room for a short time. Hannah, their daughter, had her own home.

That evening the three of us enjoyed an Indian take-away meal and several glasses of wine. I was then shown the bedroom allocated to me and, tired from my day of travelling, I slept peacefully.

The following morning, Trefor drove us to Heathrow Airport and we said our goodbyes to him. On board the plane, we settled in for our flight to JFK Airport. I think we were both anxious about what was in front of us, though we did not express it to each other. What kind of audiences would we face? How would they respond to our own poems and our readings of works by Dylan Thomas? Would the tour be a success and justify Stan's two years of planning and diligent work? We had much to think about on our long journey.

Stan and I had corresponded since 2001, when Vince Clemente had asked me for a full-length collection of my poems, which he wanted to submit to Stan for possible publication. Vince and I had corresponded since November 1997 when I had made a ten days poetry reading tour of New York and New Jersey, organised by the late Patricia Hochron, a Welsh woman who had lived in New York for decades and had worked in Upper West Side, Manhattan. One of my readings was at an Irish café, An Beal Bocht, in the Bronx, with African-American Blues poet and professor at SUNY, Raymond R. Patterson. Raymond had told Vince about me and Vince and I started to exchange long letters to each other. Almost seventeen years of those letters, poem manuscripts of mine, photos etc. are housed in the Vince Clemente Archive at Rochester University, New York.

Stan had originally planned some readings for me in America as a result of his publishing my first American book, *The Lizard Catchers*, in 2006, but during a phone call between us I mentioned I was going to see Aeronwy at the Dylan Thomas Centre in Swansea, where she was giving a reading, and to also meet with another friend of mine, Martin Holroyd, her Nottingham-based British publisher. It was not long before Stan was inspired to think about organizing a Dylan Thomas Tribute Tour, featuring Aeronwy and me.

In 2006, after the publication of my book *The Lizard Catchers*, Stan and Bebe came to Wales and I showed them the tourist sites associated with Dylan Thomas. He gave a superb reading to over one hundred people at the Dylan Thomas Centre, which Aeronwy attended. Stan and Bebe were based at the Marriott Hotel and Aeronwy and I, along with Martin Holroyd, her English publisher, met them there so that Stan could do some initial editing of her manuscript for her forthcoming book, *Burning Bridges*.

Stan and his wife Bebe met us at the Arrivals area in JFK International Airport. We were in America. It was great to see Stan and Bebe again; and, after our warm greetings and hugs, tired and a bit grubby, we dragged our suitcases and shouldered our hand luggage to Stan's car in the airport car-park. We chatted as we were driven to Merrick, Long Island, to Casa Barkan, their home and our base for the tour, Stan telling us detailed information about the latest developments for our working visit. After Aeronwy's and my seemingly forever communicating about the tour back home, here we were ready to cross America under the banner of her famous father's name. We were ready to begin at the beginning.

TUESDAY, APRIL 1: LONG ISLAND

Arrival at Casa Barkan, Merrick, New York, home of Stanley H. Barkan and Bebe Barkan, artist, the Long Island base for the entire tour.

Casa Barkan is not just the home of Stan and Bebe, it is the ever-working engine of Cross-Cultural Communications. It is a visual testament to the almost half century of Stan's amazing production of the publication of hundreds of books, primarily poetry in over fifty worldwide languages. Translation and bilingual books is at the heart of Stan's work. The CCC "family" of authors is very impressive and it includes books by the likes of Allen Ginsberg and American Poet Laureate Stanley Kunitz. There are books wherever one looks in Casa Barkan. It is the organised chaos of a busy publisher's life. Phones are always ringing and a fax machine is frequently printing. The house is a beautiful "Aladdin's Cave" of books, Bebe's stunning and original paintings, dolls, antiques, stained-glass pieces, decorated Mexican-style chairs, and their collections of ornaments and arte-facts from their many travels around the world, much of those travels connected with them furthering the CCC cause: to build bridges between different cultures, languages and literatures. At the time, Stan's beloved and now much missed cat, Pumpernickel, stalked around the various rooms.

We carried our luggage upstairs and I was allocated the ex-bedroom of one of their married children. Aeronwy was allocated the bedroom called "The Asia Room" because of its Asian ornaments and framed Asian paintings on the walls. Back downstairs, Stan showed us a large poster version of the official tour photo of us, which he planned to display with our poetry books at events. He also gave us a packet of postage stamps of our official photo that he had had produced. I was impressed by the novelty of the latter and I could not wait to send some postcards to my wife and children back in Wales. We had almost two days to recover from our jetlag and acclimatise to our new surroundings before our first event.

WEDNESDAY, APRIL 2: LONG ISLAND

Rest from overseas trip.

Stan went through the tour schedule with us and pointed out last-minute details to some of our events. Aeronwy and I then explored parts of Merrick and we discovered two places that became favourites of ours whilst on Long Island, Starbucks and Trader Joe's, a large grocery store. Our walks to Starbucks, for hot cups of English breakfast tea, sometimes a cake treat to ourselves, and where I checked my emails on my laptop, became a regular thing when our mornings were free from commitments. We would then walk as far as Trader Joe's, to get some exercise.

Aeronwy was planning to do some work on a book of memoirs, which would eventually be published as *My Father's Places: A Memoir by Dylan Thomas's Daughter* in 2009, whilst on the tour. On our leisure walks and tea stops at Starbucks, indeed during our travels across America, she would share some thoughts with me about her father and her mother. I, like her, certainly hoped to write some poems and prose inspired by our forthcoming adventures.

Aeronwy and Bebe Barkan, artist and wife of Stanley H. Barkan, in Casa Barkan.
© 2008 Peter Thabit Jones

THURSDAY, APRIL 3: LONG ISLAND

9.15 am-9.30 am: 15-minute Interview with Kathie Russo, IN THE MORNING WITH BONNIE GRICE, Southampton College radio station, WLIU.
11 am-1 pm: Videotaping of Aeronwy and Peter reading their poems by Michael Mart for www.poetryvlog.com
6 pm: Private, by invitation only, welcoming book party at Casa Barkan. The visiting poets will do a brief reading (a poem or two by Dylan Thomas, as well as original poems of their own). *Burning Bridges* **by Aeronwy Thomas (Cross-Cultural Communications, 2008) and** *The Lizard Catchers* **by Peter Thabit Jones (Cross-Cultural Communications, 2006). Buffet. Videotaping of the poets by Michael Mart of www.Poetryvlog.**

After almost two days of rest, we had a busy day and evening on Thursday, April 3. We were up early for breakfast and from 9.15 am to 9.30 am, Stan, Aeronwy and I did a live radio interview, via a phone, at the Casa Barkan kitchen table.

The interview went really well and we faced some questions that would recur throughout the tour: What were Aeronwy's thoughts about her father? What was it like for her to write poems as the daughter of such a famous poet? What did I feel like being a poet from the same city as Dylan Thomas? During the tour, Aeronwy often said to me, "It's difficult for you as a poet coming under the banner of Dylan Thomas". I would reply, "No, it's more difficult for you as a poet – you're his daughter".

Kathy Russo told me I sounded very young and very Welsh. Later on the tour, one woman at an event's reception for us asked me why I didn't sound as Welsh as Aeronwy. Aeronwy and I laughed when I told her back at Casa Barkan, as she had a beautifully toned and posh English-sounding accent. She could, in fact, perfectly mimic a Swansea accent and she occasionally did for a bit of fun, usually at my expense.

After the interview and cups of tea, we got our various poetry books from our luggage in our bedrooms and we settled in Stan's compact room next to the living room, where he has his personal library of all the books and chapbooks his CCC has published, his own published books with various publishers, and magazines and anthologies featuring his poems. Over the years, I have been in that room again many times and I am always truly impressed by Stan's dedication to world literature over the decades.

We were in the room to be videotaped by Michael Mart for www.Poetryvlog.com, an on-line series of various poets, predominantly American, reading their poems. Michael Mart, a gentle and easy-going man, spent from 11 am to 1 pm recording us reading our poems. It was a most enjoyable experience as Aeronwy and I took our turn to sit in a chair, in front of Stan's books, almost like a wallpaper of books behind us, to read our poems to Michael's very professional video-recording system.

Aeronwy and Stanley H. Barkan, in Casa Barkan.
© 2008 Peter Thabit Jones

Our next event was a welcoming book party at Casa Barkan, starting at 6 pm. A lot of people turned up for the event and Bebe and Stan provided a splendid buffet. There was a real buzz to the evening and Michael Mart was videoing it. Stan asked Aeronwy and me to stand and read from the balcony on top of the stairs, which gave us a kind of top-of-a-tree view of our audience. We both tried out specific poems of ours and some of those became our favourites for the rest of the tour. After our readings, we chatted with guests as we signed copies of our sold books. It was a lovely end to our first busy day. Tomorrow we would have our first main event away from Casa Barkan.

FRIDAY, APRIL 4: LONG ISLAND

7.30 pm: Reading/Reception at Walt Whitman Birthplace, in cooperation with BAACA, Huntington, Long Island New York. Organised by Professor Charles Adés Fishman. Hosted by Cynthia Shor and Ray Zaccaro. Welcoming wine and cheese. Videotaping by Michael Cipot.

We arrived early at the Walt Whitman Birthplace, which is situated in West Hills, Huntington, Long Island, about a forty minutes drive from Merrick. Cynthia Shor, the Executive Director, and her team at the Birthplace greeted us warmly and she then took us on a tour of the state historic site.

It was a wonderful experience to look around the home, built by the great poet's father, Walter Whitman, around 1816. Two floors and an attic, it really felt as it if we had entered into the past and the Whitman family had just gone out for the day. We returned to the Interpretive Center where a fascinating exhibition, such as portraits of Whitman, original letters and manuscripts resides and where the large performance space with a stage is located. We would soon take to the stage after a most welcome reception.

Professor and Long Island poet, Charles Adés Fishman, the organiser of our event, was present and we had attracted a good-sized crowd. We gave our readings, including readings of some of Dylan's poems and our rehearsed sections from *Under Milk Wood*. Throughout the tour, Aeronwy would tend to read *Fern Hill*, *The hand that signed the paper*, and *And death shall have no dominion*. I tended to read *The force that through the green fuse drives the flower* and *Do not go gentle into that good night*. We did, though, read other favourites of her father's poems at particular venues across America. I did the famous opening of *Under Milk Wood*, which Aeronwy had suggested I do back in Swansea, we did Mr. and Mrs. Pugh, and Aeronwy did a marvelous Polly Garter. I finished our sections from Dylan's "A Play for Voices" by reading the Reverend Eli Jenkins' prayer. Among her poems that Aeronwy read were *Later than Laugharne*, *Daughter*, *Street Lamp*, and *Night Watch*. I included my poems *Stones*, *My Grandfather's Razor*, *Rat*, and *Snow, Guitar, Lorca* among the poems I read.

The Q & A session that followed our readings was lively from a very appreciative audience. As was the case with the rest of the tour, Aeronwy answered personal questions about her father and sometimes her mother, and I answered the questions about the craftsmanship in his work. We both felt our approach worked and we were never asked a question throughout the tour that we could not answer. The evening was videoed by Michael Cipot.

After a book-signing session, we chatted with audience members and we posed for photos with Cynthia Shore and her lovely staff. One, with Walt Whitman lookalike Daniel Blaine Ford, became one of our favourite photos of the tour. Our first event at a major venue was over and Stan, Aeronwy, and I were very pleased with the way the evening had unfolded.

The Questions and Answers session.
© 2008 Peter Thabit Jones

The book signing session at Walt Whitman Birthplace.
© 2008 Peter Thabit Jones

With Cynthia Shore and her staff.
© 2008 Peter Thabit Jones

With Walt Whitman lookalike Daniel Blaine Ford.
© 2008 Peter Thabit Jones

SATURDAY, APRIL 5: NEW JERSEY

10 am-Noon: Workshop at Hamilton Club House, Paterson, New Jersey.
1 pm: Reading. Then dinner.
Hosted by Maria Mazziotti Gillan, Director of The Poetry Center at Passaic County Community College.

We were up early for our event at the Poetry Center at Passaic County Community College. We took it in turns to shower and, once dressed, we loaded our files and books, including Stan's heavy suitcase of our books for sale, into the trunk of his car. He drove us to Paterson, New Jersey, a trip of just under two hours. Aeronwy and I took in our surroundings as Stan told us amusing stories about some of his escapades around the world as a visiting publisher and poet.

Stan parked the car and we carried our stuff to the Hamilton Building. We were welcomed happily by renowned poet Maria Mazziotti Gillan, Director of the Poetry Centre, her fellow poet and her dear friend, Laura Boss, and Maria's staff, including Smita Desai.

We grabbed coffees and then I was taken upstairs to a room where I would do my writing workshop with one group, whilst Aeronwy stayed downstairs and was shown the room where she would lead her writing workshop. With my group, I discussed aspects of the craft of poetry, which were on handouts I gave them and I showed them various poetic forms, also on handouts. I then gave them some photos to stimulate ideas as they tried out some of the poetic forms. We both enjoyed working with our groups and we felt our participants produced some fine work.

At 1 p.m., after being introduced by Maria, Aeronwy and I took to the stage to give our readings. We had a full audience in the large room at the Poetry Center and there was a lively atmosphere before we started reading. Our performances were filmed by Poetry Works (USA) and for a television program, created by Maria, for airing on cable television. Aeronwy and I would eventually receive a CD copy of it. We were followed by an open mic session by some members of the audience, including those who had joined our writing workshop groups.

When the event was over, we carried our stuff to Stan's car and he followed Maria and Laura in Maria's car to a restaurant for dinner. We exchanged signed books with Maria and Laura, and Laura very kindly gave Aeronwy and I gifts. Mine was a small silver box, ideal for keeping people's business cards in it. Engraved on the lid was: Dylan Thomas Tribute Tour: April-May 2008. I was touched by such a thoughtful gesture. After our goodbyes, we headed back to Casa Barkan. I would see Maria and Laura many times on my future poetry reading visits to New York and New Jersey and I think of them as very dear friends.

MARIA MAZZIOTTI GILLAN

I had the privilege of hosting Peter Thabit Jones and Aeronwy Thomas, the poet and daughter of Dylan Thomas, at the Poetry Center at Passaic County Community College (PCCC) in Paterson, New Jersey during April and May of 2008. Aeronwy and Peter had come from Wales to the United States to participate in poetry readings and workshops while on the Dylan Thomas Tribute Tour.

I first encountered Aeronwy and Peter in Wales the previous year through the intercession of Stanley Barkan of Cross-Cultural Communications. He had arranged for Laura Boss and me to travel to Wales for a reading tour in Swansea and Laugharne, both places associated with Dylan Thomas and his work. For me, it was thrilling to be visiting the places that I had only read about in Dylan Thomas' poems, to have the opportunity to read in his childhood home as well as in the Dylan Thomas Centre in Swansea and also at Laugharne, the house where his family had been living before Thomas toured the United States prior to his death.

It was exciting to go to Fern Hill and to visit the park that was the site of Thomas' poem, "The Hunchback in the Park," but more exciting than anything was to have an opportunity to talk with Aeronwy and

Peter who shared anecdotes about Dylan Thomas, his life and work. Ever since I was a girl, I have loved Dylan Thomas' work and I remember, while in college, going to the White Horse Tavern in order to feel connected to him, to sit amid the same tables where I could imagine he had sat throughout those long evenings during his New York visits.

It was no wonder that when Stanley Barkan called to propose that I host Aeronwy and Peter during their tour that I immediately reciprocated. Their reading at The Poetry Center became their second stop while on their U.S. tour. It was a very exciting event because people were really interested in Aeronwy and her relationship with her father, her own exquisite work, as well as Peter's poetry and his wealth of knowledge about Dylan Thomas. It was exciting to watch the interaction between the audience, Peter, and Aeronwy. The benefit of their visit to The Poetry Center sparked a renewed interest in Dylan Thomas and in these two Welsh poets who were determined to bring attention to Dylan Thomas and his work.

After the reading, we held a dinner at Puzo's restaurant in Hawthorne, New Jersey, which included Peter, Aeronwy, Stanley Barkan, Laura Boss and me. It was an exciting jumble of conversation and laughter, recollections of our trip in Wales, and also a fascinating discussion of the other places that these two planned to visit across the country as part of this reading tour.

The year following their event at the Poetry Center, I was able to join Peter and the others in New York City for a walking tour of Dylan Thomas' New York haunts in Greenwich Village. We all had a chance to read a poem in honor of Dylan Thomas and at each place on the tour, we heard about its connection to Dylan and his life in New York. For me, as a long admirer of Dylan Thomas' work, this was a very exciting period and it led to another trip to an International Poetry Festival at the Dylan Thomas Theatre and to return visits to the United States by Peter as a writer-in-residence in Big Sur, California and other venues, which gave him the opportunity to write more of his own poetry and plays.

Although Aeronwy passed away the following year, I will always be grateful to have gotten to know her and her work and to have spent time with her, both in Wales and in the United States. In 2010, Cross-Cultural Communications in conjunction with Peter's The Seventh Quarry Press put out a chapbook called *Nightwatch,* a poet-to-poet collaboration of my own poems with those of Aeronwy Thomas.

Peter returned to America in 2010, where I hosted him with Stanley Barkan at Binghamton University. I feel privileged to have become friends with Peter and to have had my own work published by The Seventh Quarry and to have published both Peter and Aeronwy in the *Paterson Literary Review.* Peter is also a featured poet on a DVD produced by Poetry Works, U.S.A. for the PCCC Poetry Center. I would be remiss if I didn't mention how important Stanley Barkan and Cross-Cultural Communications were in this pairing and the opportunity he gave to all of us to celebrate Dylan Thomas and to forge this international collaboration.

Laura Boss, Maria Mazziotti Gillan, Aeronwy, Peter, and Stanley H. Barkan at the Poetry Center, Paterson, New Jersey.
© 2008 Peter Thabit Jones

Maria Mazziotti Gillan, Stanley H.Barkan, Peter, Aeronwy
and Laura Boss in Paterson, New Jersey.
© 2008 Peter Thabit Jones

LAURA BOSS AT THE PCCC READING IN PATERSON

In the photo Aeronwy, Peter, Stanley, Maria, and I are standing at the podium where Peter and Aeronwy have just read. In the background of this second floor room of historic Hamilton House is the bust of Alexander Hamilton founder of Paterson and one of Benjamin Franklin. We are all in a jovial mood in this moment in time after Peter and Aeronwy's readings. Perhaps it is the enthusiastic response of the large audience who has just heard Peter and Aeronwy read. Peter is probably happy at being called by Stanley as well as others the "successor to Dylan Thomas".

    Aeronwy has mesmerized the audience with not only her own work but also her comments and memories of her father. I can't help but wonder how she so nimbly balances the coat of her father's fame that cannot help but affect so many fans of Dylan Thomas with her own strong but feminine personality and her work that has her own signature powerful voice. So many poets are star struck whether it be on a legendary and extraordinary poet like Dylan Thomas or a singer like Bob Dylan. But Aeronwy somehow has no problem exuding her own personality separate from that of her father though physically her halo of wild curls is reminiscent of her father. But my mind and I thought perhaps Maria's as well kept drifting back to the last time I had seen Aeronwy when Maria and I were invited to read at the Dylan Thomas Centre in Swansea as well as Dylan Thomas' Boathouse in Laugharne with Aeronwy and how Peter and Aeronwy had been so hospitable as Peter drove us all over the area, and Aeronwy and Peter took us to the house her father had been born in as well as their house in Laugharne where she grew up and the shack where her father wrote and where she brought him lunch each day but never disturbed him as he wrote. We went to Fern Hill as well as the cemetery where he and Caitlin are buried together (she on top), and all the time she regaled us with stories about her father – stories only a daughter would know about her father and family. We had a reading at that house in Laugharne, and I remember being grateful for the cooperative spirit between Stanley and Peter who had arranged this reading tour of Wales.

One thing I remember thinking is how sometimes in poetry (and perhaps in life) you connect with an individual though you may not see each other again for a long time. I felt that connection with Aeronwy as we toured Wales and shared meals. She told me about her father, her mother, her childhood, which I'm sure she shared with many others. What seemed to spark that initial bond was the skirt I was wearing in Wales that Aeronwy kept telling me she just loved. My skirt, a brown silk paisley midi with a handkerchief by Ralph Lauren that I had bought at the Century 21 outlet (before it closed) had a retail Collection tag attached of $750 but had been reduced to a $28 clearance tag at this outlet. Apparently, Aeronwy recognized quality in clothes–and, of course, much more.

But in the photo for this reading at the Poetry Center in Paterson, with Peter, Stanley, Maria, and me in my usual black poetry uniform, Aeronwy is wearing a brown silk paisley long skirt so similar to the one I had worn in Wales but without the handkerchief hem, and she mentioned her skirt to me and we smiled in a way that female friends often do when they share a moment of empathetic recognition.

That was the last time I would ever see Aeronwy before she died. But sometimes I look at that photo of her at the reading in Paterson, whilst on tour with Peter, and when I see her wearing that brown paisley skirt, I cannot help but smile.

Laura Boss.
© 2019 Laura Boss

SUNDAY, APRIL 6: LONG ISLAND

1 pm: Reading, followed by a Q & A and Book Signing session, wine and cheese reception at The Stevenson Academy of Fine Arts, Oyster Bay, Long Island, New York. Hosted by Annabelle Moseley, Poet-in-Residence. Sponsored and in memoriam of Attila Hejja. Videotaping by Michael Mart of www.Poetryvlog.

It was another early start for our event at The Stevenson Academy of Fine Arts. Stan drove us to Oyster Bay, which is on the North Shore of Long Island and about a twenty minutes drive from Merrick. Our host was Annabelle Moseley, a young poet who was already making a name for herself on the American poetry scene and the Academy's poet-in-residence at the time. Michael Mart of www.Poetryvlog was there to videotape the event, which was in memoriam of Attila Hejja, the founder of the academy who had recently died. His sister, Aggie Geoghegan, had taken over the running of the Academy.

There was a wine and cheese reception before Aeronwy and I did our readings. We both tried out a few different poems of our own on this particular audience. The warm and friendly audience gave us ripples of applause after the Q & A session, which I think we were both beginning to enjoy as a part of the events, as our confidence grew in giving our replies. As the tour continued, we sometimes used humour, Aeronwy's dry and mine sometimes mischievous, to deflate awkward or odd questions. Aeronwy took everything in her stride and carried the weight of her father's extraordinary fame with dignity. He had touched so many lives in America with his dazzling writing skills, be it the serious poems of his early and later career, or the wicked Welsh humour of *Under Milk Wood*. I was very keen to help to return Dylan back to his rightful place as a remarkable craftsman in poetry and away from the popular image as the 'bar room boyo'. As he had said, "I labour by singing light". The key word being labour; and as his close friend and fellow Welsh poet Vernon Watkins had stated, "Cold craftsmanship is the best container of fire"

Annabelle Moseley and Aeronwy.
© 2008 Peter Thabit Jones

Peter, Annabelle, Stan, and Aeronwy.
© 2008 Peter Thabit Jones

We then sat at a table to sign our sold books. After taking our event stuff back to Stan's car in a nearby car-park, we headed for a celebration meal with Annabelle and her mother at a rather lively restaurant. Stan was always good at recommending particular meals to Aeronwy and me, though the fact I did not eat meat (and had not for thirty years) became a bit of a standing tease between him and me.

MONDAY, APRIL 7: NEW YORK

6.30 pm-8 pm: Reading at the Wales International Center, headquarters of the Welsh Assembly Government in North America, in the Chrysler Building, New York. Hosted by Catrin Brace, External Relations.

Trefor, Aeronwy's husband, a tenor with the London Welsh Chorale, had arrived from the UK and he became a part of our events for the next ten days. He kindly gave me one of his red Welsh rugby scarves and a bottle of port, which I kept in my bedroom at Casa Barkan and

I enjoyed having a glass or two during our leisure breaks. In the morning, he joined Aeronwy and me on our walk to Starbucks for tea and then onward for a bit of exercise to Trader Joe's. The trees were in blossom and it was a pleasant morning. We brought Trefor up to date with the tour so far.

We set off for our event at the Wales International Centre early so that Stan could find a suitable parking place on the Eastside of Midtown Manhattan. Bebe, Stan's artist wife, joined us. It took us just under an hour to get to Manhattan, the heart of the 'Big Apple' and New York City's most densely populated borough. The Wales International Centre was then situated in the Chrysler Building, an Art Deco-style building that stands like a rocket in skyscraper-crowded Manhattan.

We had been allocated official passes to allow us to go up to the floor that housed the Center. Catrin Brace, External Relations, gave us a lovely Welsh welcome. She had been the Welsh government's official host to many of the great cultural celebrities of Wales doing wonderful things in America over the years and she was responsible for organising major events to promote Wales in America, so I personally felt it was a real honour to be involved in an event that she had agreed to put together. I also felt very humbled to be reading at a venue in America representing the country of my birth.

Stan and Bebe set up their impressive book display on a table beyond the seating area. The large poster of Aeronwy and me was placed on an easel at the front of the rows of seats and behind it was an American flag on a pole. A Welsh flag on a pole stood on the other side of a translucent lectern. I was pleased to see in a glass display-cabinet two stained-glass tiles by international Swansea stained-glass artist Catrin Jones. There was also an information card in the cabinet about her. Catrin Jones had incorporated my poem *Kilvey Hill* into a full stained-glass window in the atrium of the new Saint Thomas Community School in Eastside Swansea, which had opened in 2007.

We had time before the event to explore the nearby area and have something to eat. People thronged the streets and avenues as yellow cabs dashed back and forth on the traffic-jamming wide roads. The place was one big buzz of urban humans, residents, workers, and tourists, all caught up in the colourful festival of daily activities.

Members of the Saint David's Society of New York were present at our early evening event and Catrin introduced Aeronwy, Trefor, and me to the audience. Aeronwy delighted them with her very presence, even before she began to start reading. Trefor, who sang the Reverend Eli Jenkins' prayer from *Under Milk Wood*, fitted in perfectly to our presentation. There was something very special in us performing in such an iconic building. The questions from the audience were most interesting and I mentioned aspects of cynghanedd, the strict Welsh-language poetic devices, and the use of them by English poet-priest Gerard Manley Hopkins and the acclaimed Welsh-language poet Alan Llwyd, an acknowledged master of cynghanedd, when replying to one question. It was Alan, in fact, who introduced me to cynghanedd devices when we would meet for a lunchtime drink in Swansea in the 1970s when he worked for a publisher based in the city.

We would see Catrin Brace again for our final tour event, a visit to the Greenwich Village haunts of Dylan Thomas, on May 4th. When we arrived back in Casa Barkan, Stan realised we had left the large poster of Aeronwy and me at the Center. The following day, another free day, Trefor returned to the Chrysler Building and retrieved it for our remaining East Coast events.

The room in the Chrysler Building in preparation for our event.
© 2008 Peter Thabit Jones

Stan and Bebe at their book display.
© 2008 Peter Thabit Jones

CATRIN BRACE

I was first introduced to Aeronwy Thomas and Peter Thabit Jones by Stanley Barkan who was arranging a poetry tour for them in America and asked me if the Welsh Government would sponsor a reading with them at the Wales International Center in the Chrysler Building. I, of course, agreed gladly. Stanley called me on their arrival in New York and put Aeronwy on the phone with me. In the most charming way possible, she there and then negotiated a higher fee for the two of them for their Chrysler Building appearance. I warmed to her immediately and we became good friends from then on. The evening itself was a great success, Aeronwy and Peter each reading from their own work and adding their own colour to the event.

As the Head of Marketing for the Welsh Government in New York, I was naturally keen to promote the connections between Dylan Thomas and Manhattan. I came up with the idea of a 'Dylan Thomas Walking Tour of Greenwich Village' and worked with Aeronwy and Peter to write and produce it. The tour could be run as a guided tour and was also published as a self-guided tour online and later as an app. Aeronwy and Peter participated in the inaugural tour on May 4, 2008. At the end of the tour, in Dylan's beloved White Horse Tavern, I introduced them both to David Slivka, a close friend of Dylan's and the sculptor who made his death mask. It was the first time for Aeronwy to meet David and I was very excited to make the introduction. I took a photo of Aeronwy sitting at the bar in the exact same spot as her father had sat for a photo many years previously. She quickly grabbed a pint of beer from an astonished nearby drinker so that she could look just like her father in his picture. The photo of Dylan hangs on the wall of the tavern and now Aeronwy's photo also has pride of place nearby.

After Aeronwy's sad and untimely death, it was a great pleasure to meet her daughter Hannah and to work with her in New York in 2014 during Dylan's centenary celebrations. It was Hannah who launched the Dylan Thomas Walking Tour app during the centenary.

It has been a great pleasure to work with both Aeronwy and Peter in the USA. I was always thrilled to hear Aeronwy talk about her father and her mother Caitlin and I equally enjoyed her reading from her own very lovely poetry. As a hugely talented poet, it has been an honour to work with Peter over the years and to help promote several books of his poetry in the USA. The memories will remain with me forever.

Catrin Brace leading Aeronwy, Peter and other invited guests around Greenwich Village.
© 2008 Catrin Brace

TUESDAY, APRIL 8: LONG ISLAND

Free day.

Whilst Trefor was in Manhattan, Aeronwy and I did our usual walk to Starbucks, for tea, and then on to Trader Joe's. We then walked in the other direction to call into the CVS pharmacy for some things, where one woman behind the counter was intrigued by my accent in particular. "Irish? Scottish? Belgian?" she asked. "No, Welsh," I replied. "Like Tom Jones, the singer," I added. This kind of thing occurred across America and we both always found it very amusing.

We returned to Casa Barkan to prepare for our next event in New York. That night, Aeronwy, Trefor, Stan, Bebe, and I went for an evening meal at a local restaurant, La Piazza on Merrick Road. Stan, we would come to realize, was an expert when it came to the best restaurants in the area; and over the weeks at Casa Barkan we would experience some first-class meals that represented a variety of cultures.

WEDNESDAY, APRIL 9: NEW YORK

6.30 pm-8 pm: Multilingual reading of poems by Dylan Thomas, Aeronwy Thomas, and Peter Thabit Jones at Mid-Manhattan Library, The New York Public Library, New York. Originally organized by Richard Reyes-Gavilan, Former Head, Mid-Manhattan Library Humanities Department. Hosted by Mathew Steven Baiotto. Languages and translators: Arabic (Fuad Attal), Bengali (Hassanal Abdullah), Catalan (August Bover, Mari Manent, Kristine Doll), Dutch (Leo Vroman, Georgine Sanders), French (Beverly Matherne), German (Silvia Kofler), Hebrew (Orna Rav-Hon), Italian (Marco Scalabrino, Gaetano Cipolla), Japanese (Naoshi Koriyama), Korean (Kay Richards), Portuguese (Roy Cravzow, Gregory Rabassa), Romanian (Olimpia Iacob), Russian (Aleksey Dayen), Serbian (Jamina Stojomir), Sicilian (Marco Scalabrino, Gaetano Cipolla), Spanish (Tino Villanueva, Isaac Goldemberg), Tagalog (Luisa A. Igloria), Turkish (Talât Sait Halman).

The four of us arrived at the Mid-Manhattan Library, the New York Public Library well before the starting time of 6.30 pm. Stan, as usual, wanted to make sure he found a good parking place. Our host, Mathew Steven Baiotto, took us upstairs to a large hall-size room. Stan set up his book display at the back of the hall and to the side of the rows and rows of chairs. A wooden lectern, with two microphones attached, stood in front of the seating area. To the left of the lectern, there was a table and two chairs for Aeronwy and me to sign sold books after the readings.

Aeronwy and I were looking forward to this event, to hear her father's poems and some of our poems read in so many languages, some read by the translators and some read by readers on behalf of the translators. I was excited because I would meet for the first time, emeritus professor, critic, and poet Vince Clemente.

Vince was the Consultant Editor: America of my magazine, *The Seventh Quarry Swansea Poetry Magazine*. Vince and I had corresponded since 1997 when I did a ten days poetry reading tour of New York and New Jersey, organised by the late Patricia Hochron, a Swansea woman who had moved to live and work in New York decades before. I had read with Raymond R. Patterson, a New York professor and Blues poet at the An Beal Bocht Café in the Bronx. Raymond told Vince, a close friend of his, about me and Vince and I started corresponding on a regular basis. Our letters were always very long and focused on our total devotion to poetry. Now, twenty-one years later, all of our handwritten letters to each other, many drafts of poems of mine, photos, and other materials (including materials to do with the Dylan Thomas Tribute Tour) are in the Vince Clemente Archive at Rochester University, New York. It was Vince who put me in contact with Stan in 2001, when Vince was keen to see a collection of my poems published in America. Stan had published Vince's book *Sweeter than Vivaldi*, which Vince had dedicated to me.

Vince arrived with his wife Annie and one of their two daughters. He hugged me and said, "My Welsh brother". It was a very moving experience for us to finally meet after our eleven years of the correspondence between us. Vince asked Aeronwy if he could touch her face as it was the face her father, whose works Vince had loved since he bought Dylan's *Collected Poems, 1934-1952* when the book was published in America, once touched when she was a child. She did not mind at all and she told me later that she liked Vince and she thought he was a gentleman.

We had a large audience and Stan got Aeronwy and me to read a poem, which was followed by the translation being read. Then we read another one of our poems, followed by the translation, and so on. We did the same with some of her father's poems. Stan, like an orchestra conductor, introduced the readers of the translations, such as Hassanal Abdullah (Bengali), Silvia Kofler (German), and Fuad Attal (Arabic), so that the evening's performances gelled into a fascinating event. Trefor put the cherry on the cake with his controlled and powerful singing.

After signing books and chatting to people from the audience and our fellow participants, we once again packed our tour stuff to take to Stan's car. Vince and I said our good byes as he was too unwell with physical problems, he needed a walking-stick, to join us for a meal in the city. We were, though, joined for our meal by our host, Mathew, and Michela Musolino, a wonderful singer who specializes in the folk and roots music of Sicily, and her young daughter.

New York Public Library.
© 2008 Peter Thabit Jones

Aeronwy signing some books before the start of the event.
© 2008 Peter Thabit Jones

Reading at the New York Public Library.
© 2008 Peter Thabit Jones

Peter with Vince Clemente at the New York Public Library event.
© 2008 Peter Thabit Jones

THURSDAY, APRIL 10: LONG ISLAND

10 am: Reading featuring Aeronwy Thomas and Peter Thabit Jones, with Trefor Ellis at East Meadow Public Library, Long Island, New York. Hosted by Jude Schanzer, PR/Programme Director. Videotaping by Michael Cipot.

The car drive from Casa Barkan to the East Meadow Library was barely fifteen minutes. It was a sunny day and we received a smiling welcome from Jude Shanzer, the PR/Programming Director at the library. Michael Cipot was on hand to videotape the event. Stan set up his book display at the back of the room and a lectern and microphone stood at the front of the room, where Stan placed the large poster of Aeronwy and me. Michael Cipot went about sorting the best position for him to film us. Jude was most kind and she took care of all our needs. People started to come in and sit down, and we soon had a full audience, which comprised several well-known Long Island poets.

Aeronwy and I did our usual programme and then Trefor joined us for our sections and his singing performance of Eli Jenkins' prayer from *Under Milk Wood*. We so enjoyed this part of our programme, which gave a light and comic shade to our offerings to the public. I don't use humour in my poems and the humour in a few of Aeronwy's poems is often very subtle. As each event unfolded, Aeronwy and I felt we were becoming a tighter performing unit. We were becoming more confident in our answers to questions from the audience; and we were beginning to be able to gauge what poems of ours went down well during an event.

We acknowledged the audience's generous applause, like the pages of a thick book being loudly flipped, and then Stan called us to sign books for those already queued at his table. Stan was always amused by the fact that I never seemed to have a pen. "A poet without a pen is not a poet!" he would exclaim as he handed me one of his pens. It was always nice to chat with members of the public and get their feedback. Many would tell Aeronwy how they first came to know about Dylan Thomas, at high school or college, and many seemed enamoured by his *A Child's Christmas in Wales* and *Under Milk Wood*. Over the six weeks we would even get to meet several people who had seen Dylan perform on their campuses when they were young students. Aeronwy would always listen to their stories carefully and one sensed the pride she felt when they spoke of her father's astonishing delivery of his poems and poems by some of his favourite poets, such as W. B. Yeats and Edward Thomas.

I had created my own business cards back home in Swansea, with a package for a computer, and Aeronwy had asked me to do some for her when I had shown her one of mine. So we would often give one to people who wanted to remain in contact with us. I also had business cards for my magazine *The Seventh Quarry Swansea Poetry Magazine* and I would hand them to poets I met and invite them to submit work for my magazine.

I would get to do more readings for Jude in succeeding years when I visited New York for various events organized by Stan, and it was always a pleasure to see her again and do an event at East Meadow Public Library.

Aeronwy, Trefor, and I had the rest of the day off and so once we left our stuff at Casa Barkan, we busied ourselves by strolling around Merrick, whilst Stan tackled his urgent chores in his upstairs working room.

Stan and Aeronwy as we leave Casa Barkan for the event
at East Meadow Public Library.
© 2008 Peter Thabit Jones

FRIDAY, APRIL 11: LONG ISLAND

7 pm-9 pm: Private cocktail party, reading by Aeronwy Thomas and Peter Thabit Jones, Q&A and book-signing session, by invitation only at the home of Jane and Ken Schwartz. Poets interviewed by Charles Fishman. Videotaping by Michael Cipot.

Ken Schwartz, Stan's radiologist cousin, and his wife Jane kindly organized this private event at their large and opulent North Haven home in Long Island. Bebe joined us for the evening and we arrived early. We were made to feel at home by our hosts as they introduced us to those they had invited. The party food spread out on the kitchen table was more like a banquet for royalty than a welcome meal for two Welsh poets and a Welsh tenor.

We sat with the other invited guests, including Galen Williams, founder of Poets & Writers, and her partner, the elderly and famous American poet and literary critic Harvey Shapiro, enjoying our plates of delicious food and our drinks. Harvey Shapiro, I felt, had a commanding presence. During his time with *The New York Times* newspaper, from 1957 to 1995, he was Editor of *The New York Times Magazine* and *The Times Book Review*. He was very congenial and seemed genuinely interested in the tour Stan had organised for Aeronwy and me across America. It was a privilege to meet such an acclaimed literary man.

Stan, when ready to begin the main reason for the evening, told Aeronwy, Trefor, and me to stand in front of a wall in the room where our invited audience was seated. We then proceeded to do our readings and Trefor finished with his songs. Whilst with us, he sometimes sang other Welsh songs as well as the Reverend Eli Jenkins' Prayer from *Under Milk Wood*. To conclude the evening, Charles Adés Fishman, a Long Island professor and poet, interviewed Aeronwy and me. I felt the both of us gave good answers to Charles' stimulating questions.

The evening reminded me of the kind of poetry readings that poets, such as John Clare and Charlotte Mew, did in the past when they entertained wealthy people at their homes. It was another new experience for Aeronwy, Trefor, and me. Aeronwy and I would gather in many more memorable experiences as we made our way across a vast and fascinating country.

SATURDAY APRIL 12: LONG ISLAND

2 pm: Special reception for Aeronwy Thomas and Peter Thabit Jones, reading their own poetry and poetry by Dylan Thomas, with a special performance by tenor Trefor Ellis, followed by a Q&A session, and hors d'oeuvres & wine, coffee & tea, at the Southampton Inn, Shinnecock Room, Long Island, New York. Hosted by Tammy Nuzzo-Morgan, The North Sea Poetry Scene.

The drive from Casa Barkan to the Southampton Inn in Hill Street, Long Island, took us around one hour and twenty minutes. Stan and I were booked into the Southampton Inn for the night and Aeronwy and Trefor were staying with our host, Tammy Nuzzo-Morgan, well-known poet, editor, and founder of The North Sea Poetry Scene.

When I woke up, Stan had already made his way to the Shinnecock Room, where the event was taking place, to set out his book display. I showered and joined him. After breakfast, I went back to my room, to read through some of my poems for a half hour and get mentally ready for the event. An article about us had already appeared in the local newspaper and so we were all hoping for a good attendance. I gathered my books and papers and headed for the Shinnecock Room well ahead of the 2 pm start.

As I climbed the stairs to the Southampton Inn, I could hear a piano, its fresh raindrop of notes claiming the late morning, and then Trefor's Welsh voice, singing, bringing to America a folk song from our Wales. I felt a touch of *hiraeth* (a deep longing), a few weeks far from my home, as warm as a long hug from one of my children. Trefor was getting ready for the event later.

The Shinnecock Room, spacious and inviting, soon packed out with our waiting audience. There were a lot of Long Island poets, associated with The North Sea Poetry Scene, among the audience. One lady came up to me before the start and asked if I could introduce her to "Irony". It became one of our little fun stories in conversations with other people during the tour. Tammy introduced us and we delivered our performances from a platform with microphones. The audience showed their genuine appreciation for our readings and for Trefor's singing. After the Q & A session, Aeronwy and I sat at separate tables, to sign copies of our books. Aeronwy's queue was longer than mine and we laughed about it later.

As we enjoyed the hors d'oeuvres & wine, coffee & tea, various people came up to chat with us. Many people wanted to comment on or know more about Dylan Thomas, but many also had comments and questions about our poems, which for both of us was always rewarding. That evening, Stan and I made our way home. Aeronwy and Trefor stayed with Tammy for a while and she would return them to Merrick.

Stan, Peter, Tammy Nuzzo-Morgan, our host, and others after the event.
© 2008 Peter Thabit Jones

SUNDAY, APRIL 13: SALEM, MASSACHUSETTS

Depart for Salem, Massachusetts. Residing with Professor Kristine Doll.

We set off on our first long journey from Casa Barkan for our events in another American State. Our travelling involved boarding a car ferry; it was a long journey by road and car ferry, around five hours. We stopped for meals and drinks at a gas station. We were all glad to be greeted by Professor Kristine Doll, a renowned Spanish and Catalan literary translator and a widely published poet, at her very confortable home in Salem. Aeronwy, Trefor and I carried our luggage up to the third level of the tall and wooden property where we would be sleeping and Stan based himself on the second level. Kristine soon made us feel very much at home with cups of tea and various treats.

We soon got on friendly terms with Kristine's lively family of dogs, cats, and her caged birds. In front of the bedroom allocated to Aeronwy and Trefor and the bedroom allocated to me was a relaxing room with a settee, chairs, television, fridge, and microwave. The window of the room showed a part of Kristine's fenced-in garden below and the back of neighbouring houses; and the view from the windows of our bedrooms was of the tall and similar wooden properties on the other side of the street's road. It was in this room that we congregated for tea and conversations whilst staying with her.

After our settling in and refreshments, Kristine suggested she show all of us some of the shops in Salem, including one owned by a real witch. We strolled along the streets, where the houses seemed to be huddled as close as witches. She told us about the infamous purge on witches and the trials that took place in 1692 and 1693. They, of course, inspired Arthur Miller's 1953 drama, *The Crucible* and the 1996 film version of his work. Stan did not come in the witch's shop with us, which was full of feathers, cat ornaments, candles, skulls, jewelry, and artifacts: very pagan. I expected the witch to fix her eyes on us like a cat does and look into our souls, but she gave us a very happy smile.

We went for a meal early evening in a British-type pub, which was just up the road from where Kristine lives, beyond Salem Common and the Salem Witch Museum and opposite the Hawthorne Hotel, named after writer Nathaniel Hawthorne. A female friend of Kristine's joined us and we all had a good laugh and chilled out before the following day's events. We walked back to Kristine's home as night shadowed out the day. Salem Common was dark and empty. The blood-red windows of the Salem Witch Museum were eerily lit up. She told us that Halloween in Salem was a parade and that witches took over Salem, coming from everywhere.

MONDAY, APRIL 14: SALEM, MASSACHUSETTS

11 am-5 pm: Reading/Creative Writing Workshop at Salem State University. Sponsors: the School of Arts and Sciences, the college's Creative Writing Program, and the Salem Chapter of Phi Kappa Phi. Hosted by Professor Kristine Doll.

The drive from Kristine's home to the modern red bricked university was very quick. We gave our readings in a recreational area for students at the University. Our audience primarily contained those who were on the college's Creative Writing Program and some college lecturers, such as the poet J. D. Scrimmage, so we had a very observant group of people in the room. Stan had placed the large poster of Aeronwy and me on an easel. I was starting to lose my voice because of a sore throat and cold, so it was decided that Trefor would stand in for me and do the parts I usually read from *Under Milk Wood*.

After the Q & A conclusion, we took a lunch break. The Massachusetts poet Peter H. Fulton attended our event and he got talking to Aeronwy and me while we relaxed before the Creative Writing Workshop we were going to do with some of J. D. Scrimmage's students on the Creative Writing Program. Peter and I would be involved in events in Massachusetts and in Wales in the coming years. I was worried I would lose my voice altogether as we had events at Wellesley College and the historic Grolier Poetry Book Shop the following day.

After lunch, J. D. Scrimmage showed us around the campus as we headed for the classroom where we would do our workshop with his students. The students were split into two groups and Aeronwy and I worked with our allocated group. We ended the session by getting the students to read what they had written.

That evening we all went out for a meal in Salem. We would say goodbye to Kristine in the morning as we departed for Wellesley College, but we would see her again at the Grolier Poetry Book Shop event. She and I would become very dear friends and we would participate in literary translation conferences, in such places as Pennsylvania and Toronto, over the years and at the Massachusetts Poetry Festival.

Aeronwy, a colleague of Kristine's, Peter, and Kristine at Salem State University.
© 2008 Peter Thabit Jones

Trefor performing at Salem State University.
© 2008 Peter Thabit Jones

Peter at Salem State University.
© 2008 Peter Thabit Jones

KRISTINE DOLL

Displayed in front of the splendid poetry collections of Peter Thabit Jones and Stanley H. Barkan that grace my bookshelves is a photograph of Ms. Aeronwy Thomas and Mr. Thabit Jones. It is a tender, visual rendering of the relationship between the two poets that is powerful and supportive even if now imbued with sadness. In it, Mr. Thabit Jones is to the right of Ms. Thomas and is shown in profile looking towards her. Ms. Thomas gazes out at us, the viewers, with a steady, warm look that invites us to approach, as if we had just interrupted a conversation the two of them were having and yet would be welcomed to join. It is also, however, a very private moment. Mr. Thabit Jones is marked by a gentle air of melancholy as if knowing that this moment will pass all too soon.

Aeronwy died in July 2009.

I will never again hear Aeronwy's melodic accent ripple along her request for a cup of Earl Grey tea but I can hold this picture and remember her when she was here with her husband, Trefor, and with Peter and Stanley who had all come to Salem Massachusetts to read, to talk about and to teach poetry. It is hard to believe that nearly ten years have passed.

My first glimpse of Aeronwy was as she emerged, calm and dignified, from the pent-up energy in Stan's car and the five-hour journey the four of them had just undertaken from New York to Salem. We would spend the next several days together sharing insights into poetry and discussing their tour of the United States that Stan had organized. Over the meals we enjoyed, stories from our personal lives were also revealed. My house lit up with their energy and laughter. Duende, that magic spark, resided with us, keeping company with us at their poetry readings and workshops, sitting up with us late into the night, weaving its charm through all of our activities.

Salem State University, where I teach, hosted a series of readings and workshops showcasing the poetry of both Peter and Aeronwy, with special recognition of that of Dylan Thomas. Similar readings took place later in the week at the Grolier Poetry Book shop and at Harvard University's Adams House, both in Cambridge, Massachusetts.

Peter's book, *The Lizard Catchers*, had just been published and was a particular favorite of students of the Foreign Languages Department and of the Creative Writing program at Salem. I recently spoke with a graduate who asked me about Mr. Thabit Jones and remarked upon one of the poems of that collection, "Stones" that Peter had read at the university bookstore reception. He mentioned the impact that the poem had had on him so many years ago and the spiritual connection it still strengthened for him with the New England landscape, which is often one of low stone walls between large open fields or through narrow wooded tracts.

Peter's poetry and its translation into more than 20 languages were inspirational. Over the next few years, several of our students would translate Peter's verse into Spanish and so discover their own love of poetry and the music of translation. They were delighted by Peter's discussion of the craftsmanship behind so much great poetry and specifically, that of Dylan Thomas, including his use of Welsh-language devices and forms, such as *Cynghanedd*. Peter would encourage all of us to experiment with these devices and would go on to develop a series of workshops that he would later present at some of New England's most prestigious literary conferences.

Aeronwy Thomas' readings of her poetry and of her father's invited audiences to experience these sound devices through the power and melody of her voice, and the fluid rhythm of the verse of both father and daughter. As during our personal time together, Aeronwy and her husband Trefor were gracious, accessible and genuinely engaging. I recall Aeronwy's smile when she spoke about her father and led us on journeys through his poetry. I remember the direct manner with which she accompanied us into her own poetry.

I also remember hilarious stories told over lunches and dinners, often punctuated with the most unexpected witticisms, that drew us closer together than such a short amount of time would normally have permitted.

I remember all of this and am so grateful. As I hold the picture of Aeronwy and Peter, I can feel their deep friendship and support for each other and for all of us who were fortunate enough to have been with them on that memorable journey. I do my best to push away my sadness over her untimely death and look, instead, at her steady gaze and remember and thank her for allowing me to share a period of time when we laughed and joked, and talked about poetry and the world, and felt timeless.

Kristine Doll.
© 2019 Kristine Doll

TUESDAY, APRIL 15:
WELLESLEY/CAMBRIDGE, MASSACHUSETTS

1 pm-2 pm: Reading at Wellesley College, Wellesley, Massachusetts. Hosted by Ifeanyi A. Menkiti.

Wellesley College is about a one hour and twenty minute drive from Salem. Ifeanyi A. Menkiti, a Professor of Philosophy and a poet, greeted us. He is also the owner of the historic Grolier Poetry Book Shop in Cambridge, Massachusetts. We knew that Aeronwy's father had read at Wellesley College on one of his four American reading tours and so this event was special to us. We were to give our readings and Trefor was to sing in the Lulu Chow Wong Campus Center. Stan had arranged an addition to the event. A Korean student, a young woman, would read some Korean translations of our poems.

Apart from students, some professors turned up and one retired professor, after our event, told Aeronwy she had attended Dylan's reading at Wellesley as a young student. Aeronwy, as always, answered the woman's questions politely, and I could see Aeronwy was very interested in what the woman had to say about her father. I got chatting with a professor who wanted to know more about Dylan's use of sound-texturing in his poems.

We said our farewells to Ifeanyi, who we would see at our evening event and we headed for our hotel in Cambridge, the Friendly Inn, to deposit our stuff, before exploring Harvard Square and going for a meal. I hoped my voice, diminishing because of my sore throat, would be up to reading Dylan's and my poems.

Stan's book display at Wellesley College (with Aeronwy's pink coat and scarf placed on a chair).
© 2008 Peter Thabit Jones

Ifeanyi A. Menkiti, Aeronwy, and Stan.
© 2008 Peter Thabit Jones

Peter, the Korean student, who read translations of our poems, and Aeronwy.
© 2008 Peter Thabit Jones

7 pm: Reading at Adams House, Harvard, organized by the Grolier Poetry Book Shop, Cambridge, Massachusetts. Hosted by the bookshop owner Ifeanyi A. Menkiti.

We congregated at the Grolier Poetry Book Shop before the event at Harvard's Adams House. There was a poster of our event in the shop window. It was great to see Ifeanyi again and to be introduced to his wife, Carol, the shop's Special Liaison, Elizabeth Doran, the very dedicated manager, and Dan Wuenschel, who also worked there. We also met Kristine again and a few of the other poets/translators who would be participating with us at the event. We all posed for photos together, standing in front of the bookshelves.

A small shop, the Grolier oozes with literary history. Founded in 1927 by Adrian Gambet and Gordon Cairnie, it was the next owner, Louisa Solano, who steered it towards focusing solely on poetry books and poetry events. Ifeanyi bought the shop in 2006. The shop has been frequented by the likes of Seamus Heaney, Robert Pinsky, Charles Olson, Anais Nin and many others. To me, it felt very special, indeed a privilege, that Aeronwy and I were the featured poets at an event under the banner of the historic Grolier.

My voice, despite my taking medicines and tablets, was reduced to a rasping whisper slightly amplified. I really felt under the weather as we all headed for Adams House, a building just down the road from the Grolier. The place was packed out and after Ifeanyi welcomed everyone and said some things of why he felt connected to Dylan Thomas, Stan took over and introduced each supporting poet and translator, including Kristine, who read leading Catalan poet August Bover's translations of some of Aeronwy's and my poems, Tino Villanueva, who read the Spanish translations, and Pavel Grushko, who read the Russian translations. Aeronwy, Trefor, and I did our usual performances. Aeronwy gave her usual thoroughly engaging and professional reading and Trefor's rendering of some traditional Welsh songs were much appreciated by those who had come to see us.

I recall Stan asking me to read Dylan's moving *Elegy*, which someone had requested. The elegy for Dylan's father, D. J. (David John) was unfinished on Dylan's death, and Vernon Watkins, his close friend and fellow Welsh poet, eventually completed it, using Dylan's manuscript drafts of the poem. I managed to get through the beautifully crafted poem, even though I felt my voice would fail at any moment.

There was a wine and cheese buffet as we signed books for members of the audience. Another addition to the evening in Cambridge was Aeronwy being interviewed by Doug Holder, an established poet and a highly respected publisher. Arranged by Stan, it was carried out at Dunkin Donuts in Harvard Square, where we also enjoyed some refreshments. The piece appeared in *The Somerville Times*.

The Grolier Poery Book Shop, Harvard Square, Cambridge.
© 2008 Peter Thabit Jones

Peter outside the bookshop before the event.
© 2008 Peter Thabit Jones

Peter, Carol Menkiti, Dan Wuenschel, Aeronwy, Ifeanyi Menkiti, and Elizabeth Doran, Manager of the bookshop.
© 2008 Peter Thabit Jones

CAROL MENKITI

In April of 2008, Ifeanyi A. Menkiti, Wellesley College professor and owner of the historic Grolier Poetry Book Shop in Harvard Square, welcomed Peter Thabit Jones and Aeronwy Thomas to join a group of poets and translators in discussion and celebration of the life and work of Aeronwy's father, the celebrated Welsh poet Dylan Thomas. Menkiti, who hosted a poetry reading as a part of the event organized by Stanley H. Barkan of Cross-Cultural Commnications, was quoted by Doug Holder, publisher of the Ibbetson Street Press, as saying, "I love Dylan Thomas' sense of community. His work releases a poetic impulse around the world. It travels across borders." In the publication *Wellesley Week*, Menkiti added: "Whether one reads his poems alone, by oneself, or hears them read aloud by him or others, or perhaps hears read aloud the captivating words of *A Child's Christmas in Wales*, one always comes away with a sense of ineffable magic in the air–a sense that words are potent things."

The event began at the bookshop, though the reading took place later in the evening at Harvard's Adams House. Thomas' and Thabit Jones's readings of both Dylan Thomas' poetry and their own work were accompanied by a performance from Aeronwy's husband, tenor Trefor Ellis, who sang traditional Welsh folk songs and a song from Dylan Thomas's *Under Milk Wood*. Subsequent readings were by Kristine Doll, Professor of Foreign Languages at Salem State College and a translator of Catalan, who read August Bover's translations of the featured poets' work into Catalan. Pavel Grushko, translator of American, English, and Latin American poetry into Russian, read translations of the featured poets into Russian, including a translation by Aleksey Dayen. Tino Villanueva, founder of Imagine Publishers Inc., editor of *Imagine: International Chicano Poetry Journal*, read his translation of a Dylan Thomas poem into Spanish, as well as translations by Isaac Goldemberg. The event recognized and honoured the cross-cultural reception of Dylan Thomas's work, further providing a platform for engagement with contemporary Welsh poets, Peter Thabit Jones and Aeronwy Thomas.

Carol Menkiti.
© 2008 Peter Thabit Jones

WEDNESDAY, APRIL 16:
HARVARD UNIVERSITY, MASSACHUSETTS

11.45 am: visit to the Woodberry Poetry Room (in Harvard Yard) for listening to rare uncirculated tapes of Dylan Thomas reading his works.
1.15 am: visit to the Department of Public Services, Houghton Library, Harvard University, Cambridge, Massachusetts, for viewing of Dylan Thomas manuscripts. The visit is courtesy of Susan Halpert. Hosts: Leslie Morris and Rachel Howarth. These visits arranged by Professor and poet Tino Villanueva.

Our visit to Harvard's Woodberry Poetry Room and its Houghton Library was an interesting addition to our usual readings and workshops. We had our breakfast early and then our small group, guided by Tino Villanueva, made our way into Harvard Yard.

In the Woodberry Poetry Room, we all listened intently to rare recordings of Dylan Thomas reading some of his works, including his *A Visit to America*, a short and very humorous piece. In fact, it is the only piece, apart from letters to family and friends, that he wrote about his four visits to America. We sat, listening to the iconic Welsh voice, powered by elocution lessons as a child, booming around the room. That hypnotic voice, rhythmic and magical, that had mesmerized audiences across America, whilst Caitlin, Llewellyn, Aeronwy, and Colm carried on with their lives back in The Boathouse in Laugharne; and now Aeronwy and I were in America and she was sat quietly, hearing her father deliver his offerings to those who had attended his events.

We moved on to the Houghton Library, where we were shown photos never seen beyond the confines of the library. I recall one photo of Dylan with Oscar Williams, an American poet and editor and a friend who found places for some of Dylan's poems in American magazines. Oscar usually tried to get a good fee for Dylan from such magazines.

Aeronwy never said to me what she really felt about listening to her father's voice whilst in the country where he tragically died, or her thoughts about seeing unpublished photos of him. It was, though, at this time that she started to think about a poem that would eventually become *The Shade*, which would be drafted properly when we were based in a motel in Chicago. At breakfast in that motel, she showed the poem to me and asked for my suggestions. My suggestion was that the last line should be "dogs my steps", which would allude to her father's wonderful collection of stories, *Portrait of the Artist as a Young Dog*, which was his pun on James Joyce's *Portrait of the Artist as a Young Man*. She took my advice.

Even before the tour, Aeronwy would sometimes send me a letter and a poem and ask for my comments. *Street Lamp*, a favourite poem of mine by her, was one. Later on the tour, when I drafted a poem about our time in Boulder, Colorado, she gave me valuable advice about the last stanza, which I altered.

After our pleasant and relaxing visit to Harvard, our small group went for a farewell Chinese meal at a nearby restaurant, before we were soon back on the road again in the late afternoon and heading back to our Long Island base.

Aeronwy in Cambridge, Boston.
© 2008 Peter Thabit Jones

Peter in Harvard Yard.
© 2008 Peter Thabit Jones

TINO VILLANUEVA

AERONWY THOMAS' VISIT TO THE GROLIER BOOK SHOP

To have had in our midst a decade ago, Aeronwy Thomas (1943–2009), the daughter of none other than Dylan Thomas (1914–1953)–accompanied by Welsh poet Peter Thabit Jones, was an exciting literary event for many, and for me personally. I had already met Aeronwy in June of the previous year in Swansea, Wales, when Beverly Matherne and I had read at the Dylan Thomas Centre and the Dylan Thomas Boat House, readings sponsored by Thabit Jones's journal, *The Seventh Quarry*. I had found Aeronwy to be warm, well-disposed, and softspoken, with a quiet charm very much her own. Thus, when I received word from Stanley Barkan, my New York editor at Cross-Cultural Communications, that a U. S. reading tour was being contemplated for Aeronwy and Peter, and that on April 15, 2008 they would be the featured readers at the venerable Grolier Poetry Book Shop in Cambridge, Massachusetts, I set about to organize a couple of events that would further enhance, I reasoned, their brief visit to the Boston area.

What I envisioned was two-fold, and can best be summarized by the E-mail below addressed to Stanley. First, to have the honored guests visit the Woodberry Poetry Room at Harvard University with the purpose of listening to two cassette-tape recordings of Dylan Thomas reading both from his work and from that of other poets, recorded on March 2, 1950 (Harvard University reading), and May 11, 1953 (Massachusetts Institute of Technology reading). Attending would be Aeronwy, Peter, Stanley, and Ifeanyi Menkiti, the owner of the Grolier Poetry Book Shop, who was hosting their reading later that evening at Adams House [Harvard University], a few steps down the street from the Grolier.

Still within Harvard Yard, and just to the left of Lamont Library, where the Woodberry Poetry Room is housed, sits the Houghton Library, a repository where some of Dylan Thomas' papers are archived. There, too, I arranged through one of the librarians, Ms. Susan Halpert, to have on display for our special visitors: manuscripts, drafts of poems, never-before-published photographs, letters from Dylan's wife Caitlin, publicity releases, etc. The following paragraphs from my E-mail to Stanley Barkan spell out my intentions. Said letter was sent from my office in the Department of Romance Studies, Boston University, where I was teaching at the time:

Boston, 29 January 2008

Dear Stan,

I went to the Houghton Library (in Harvard Yard) today to inquire about the possibility of seeing the Dylan Thomas MSS. when Peter and Aeronwy are here. The reference librarian I saw agreed to bring them out for us to see on April 15. She asked if we just wanted to look at them, or if we would be commenting on them as well. If the latter, we cannot be in the reading / research room, so she said she could book us in "the green room" off to the side of a larger hall. I said, we'll take it. I mentioned that about six of us would probably be present. I'm supposed to confirm all of this with her about one week to ten days before the April 15 date.

She also brought up that if we wanted to look at other related material such as that in the [John] Keats and [Emily] Dickinson rooms we could request it. We'll get a brief tour, was my understanding. I said, yes, why not? Ms. Susan Halpert expects us between 10:00 am and 12:00 noon, but said it would be ideal if we could be there closer to 10:00 am, for there are other activities already scheduled that staff has to tend to closer to noon. (I would say that if we're there between 10:15–10:30, that would be fine. I don't see ourselves being there more than an hour.

From there we'll walk next door (still within Harvard Yard) to the Woodberry Poetry Room to listen to (not all, I suppose) the Thomas tapes of the readings he did at M. I. T. and Harvard on two of his visits here. (You can google the Woodberry and see what they have on Thomas.) I was told minutes later at the Grolier Book Shop that I better re-establish contact with the Woodberry, because the person I'd spoken to in August is no longer there, and so I'll have to do the arranging all over again. I shall take care of this next week at the latest.

[...]

Ok, Stan, I have to get back to preparing [for class] for tomorrow. I'd like to go home in an hour and prepare myself a frozen margarita, or some Spanish cream sherry, and have a bite to eat.

Sincerely, Tino

Aeronwy, after having heard Dylan reading with such brio on the tapes, remarked that behind her father's gusto for words, and his resonant enunciation of them in the poems he read, was his early training as a dramatic actor. There is every reason to believe this is true–at eighteen Thomas had joined the Swansea Little Theatre in Mumbles, and, it has been commented that in one of the roles he played, he gave "a most impressive and clever representation in the view of the theater critic" (Constantine FitzGibbon: *The Life of Dylan Thomas* (Boston: Little, Brown and Company, 1965).

Altogether, I was more than delighted to have reunited daughter with father, as it were, and, in general, to have played a minor role in adding to Aeronwy Thomas's and Peter Thabit Jones's U. S. reading tour, all in the spirit of the literary for everyone involved, most especially for Aeronwy, who had never heard these audio recordings from some five-and-a-half decades prior. (These can be listened to at the Woodberry Poetry Room by members of the public; by and large, however, they remain unavailable commercially, but accessible online or through scholarly requests.) Aeronwy's passing in 2009 left a void in those of us who were privileged to have met her.*

---

*It was on the occasion of Aeronwy's visit to Cambridge that she handed me her business card, the back of which publicized two of her books, the images of their covers printed in miniaturized forms: *Rooks and Poems* (2004) and *Burning Bridges* (2008). At the reading at Adams House, Stanley Barkan served as MC and also read. Other participants including Aeronwy Thomas and Peter Thabit Jones were: Aldo Tambellini, Kristine Doll, Pavel Grushko, (Aeronwy's husband) Trevor Ellis, Aled Llion Jones, and Tino Villanueva. For a summary of that evening's proceedings, see: Doug Holder: "Somerville Poets Host Dylan Thomas' Daughter," *The Somerville Times*, April 28, 2008.

Tino Villanueva.
© 2010 Pavel Grushko

THURSDAY, APRIL 17: NEW YORK

6.30 pm-8.30 pm: Reading at The Graduate Center, CUNY, New York. Hosted by Professor Sultan Catto.

We arrived in Manhattan in plenty of time for our reading at The Graduate Center, CUNY (City University of New York), organised by Sultan Catto, a very distinguished Physics professor and a poet. Situated in an impressive building on Fifth Avenue, the Center is a public American research institution and post-graduate university. It is the principal doctoral-granting institution of the City University of New York system. Our early arrival allowed us to do some sightseeing around Fifth Avenue and grab something to eat and drink.

Sultan got us all through the security system of the Center and took us to the room where we would give our readings. Stan's book display was set up and we all chilled out whilst waiting for our audience to enter and take their seats. It was a very large room, with windows that gave great views of the surrounding buildings and sky windows that allowed us to see the tops of various skyscrapers. Through a sky window in the room, we could actually see the Empire State Building, a minute's walk from the Center.

Our audience started to arrive and appeared to be comprised of lecturers and students. We were pleased to see we were going to read to a full room again. A wooden lectern, emblazoned with the words The Graduate Center, the City University of New York, and microphone had been set up for us alongside a table with another microphone; and Stan had placed the poster of Aeronwy and me on one of the window frames behind the lectern and table.

Aeronwy and I did our readings and Trefor sang. His singing was heartfelt and controlled. Our performances worked so well together. We were a tight unit and our dedicated practice back in Wales before the tour contributed to our gelling so well. It was yet another fabulous experience in Manhattan. Three Welsh people giving Americans a taste of Wales via poetry and song, in a room above the ever-busy evening sidewalks, the glaring neon lights, and the slow flow of bumper-to-bumper traffic down below.

Sultan was a gracious host and he and I would become close friends when I returned to Casa Barkan for events in New York. Thanks to him, I even read twice more at The Graduate Center in the years that followed, whilst stopping with him and his wife at their New Jersey home.

Trefor testing the microphone in The Graduate Center, CUNY, while Aeronwy relaxes before the event.
© 2008 Peter Thabit Jones

The Graduate Center, CUNY.
© 2008 Peter Thabit Jones

The Empire State Building viewed from The Graduate Center, CUNY.
© 2008 Peter Thabit Jones

FRIDAY, APRIL 18: NEW YORK

6 pm-8 pm: Buffet dinner, reading, Q &A session, book signing, at the Grand Gallery of The National Arts Club, New York. Co-hosted by Sharyn Grossman, Chair of the Film Committee, and Cherry Provost, Chair of the Literary Committee.

Trefor, who would be very much missed by us, departed for his journey back to the UK, as we returned to Manhattan again for our event at the celebrated National Arts Club on Gramercy Park S. Founded in 1898 by Charles DeKay, an art and literary critic of the *The New York Times*, it is a private club in the Samuel J. Tilden House, a Victorian Gothic revival building. Writers Mark Twain, W. H. Auden, and Frank McCourt were club members at one time. Current members include Robert Redford and Martin Scorsese.

It is a magnificent building inside, truly grand and palatial. The evening began with a sumptuous buffet dinner. We all sat at a long table with Sharyn Grossman, Chair of the Film Committee, and Cherry Provost, Chair of the Literary Committee, and other club dignitaries. The various tables were bubbling with conversations and a nearby bar was very busy. One sensed a special evening was in progress.

The very large room was packed with our audience. The lectern with a gold-coloured reading lamp and a microphone was set up for us. We both rose to the occasion and gave controlled and engaging readings of our poems and our chosen poems by Dylan Thomas. We did not do sections from *Under Milk Wood* for this event, which was a last minute decision by the both of us. After I read, I stood nearby and watched Aeronwy as she read. As I had thought at all our events up to that point, I wondered what the audience members were thinking as my eyes scanned the room. There they were, listening to the only daughter of Dylan Thomas reading some of his most famous poems, reading in a rich and commanding voice. She was the daughter who sometimes heard her father mumbling lines and words to himself in his writing shed above The Boathouse, as she passed it with her friends as they played. As always, the audience responded as enthusiastically to her poems as to those of her father.

I joined her for the Q & A session and we handled it with confidence. Aeronwy added some things to my response to a question and I added some things to her replies. We then made our way for the book signing area, where Stan was waiting for us. One lady told us that the actor Patrick Stewart, now of *Star Trek: The Next Generation* fame, had been at the club on March 10, to receive the 2008 Sir John Gielgud Award.

Then, once more, we headed through the city that never sleeps, a city made famous as the location for so many Hollywood films, brighter and more tantalising than a fairground at night. Aeronwy rested her head on her seat. I stared out of the window and thought of my family back home in Wales as Stan drove us to Merrick, Long Island.

Peter reading at the National Arts Club, New York.
© 2008 Peter Thabit Jones

SATURDAY, APRIL 19: MANHATTAN

Free day: the authors will visit Manhattan.

Stan dropped Aeronwy and me off at Merrick Train Station, so that we could take the Long Island Rail Road to Manhattan, about a three quarters of an hour journey. He showed us how to purchase tickets from the machine with our dollar bills. He and Bebe had already told us back at Casa Barkan where to get off, namely at Penn Station (Pennsylvania Station). He returned to Casa Barkan, though he and Bebe would be visiting relatives later on and they would not be returning home that night.

We stood, waiting with other commuters for our train to arrive. We were so looking forward to our time in Manhattan. It was a treat to our selves and the chance to really unwind from our busy schedule. We had decided we would just wander around, although Aeronwy hoped we could visit Ground Zero and I wanted to see The Dakota, where John Lennon had lived and died, which I first saw in 1997 when doing readings in New York and New Jersey. We boarded the train and chatted quietly as the train set off. Throughout the tour, we were always at ease with each other and that served us well when we slightly panicked because we had lost our way back to a host's home after a leisurely walk and such things.

A voice made announcements before each stop, so there was no chance of us getting off too soon or too late. Also, Aeronwy was always more alert than I when it came to the finer details of our travelling arrangements. I loved it when the voice on the train announced, "This is the train to Babylon" as the journey was on the Babylon Branch of the Long Island Rail Road. Years later, when I had travelled on the line several times whilst stopping with Stan and Bebe for various poetry events, I wrote a poem with the refrain, "This is the train to Babylon".

We made our way through the daily bustle of commuters in Penn Station, until we found the exit to Lexington Avenue, where we joined the real-life film-set that is Manhattan. We walked among the hectic flow of people. It was if all the world's races were out and about in the city. We heard the jabber of many different languages. The intriguing parade of the day came and went in the eyes' quick dream. All was NOW. Skyscrapers stood in their paradise of mammon moments. Car horns blamed each other in the slow metal river of traffic, as the roads let off their built-up steam. I wondered when did the city take a break to ease its anxious heart.

It was a warm and sunny day and we visited many of the obvious tourist places. We were amused by some of the things on sale in the famous Macy's department store. We stood opposite the Hard Rock Café. As we walked towards pedestrian-packed Times Square, I was impressed by a huge billboard advertisement for the film *Indiana Jones and the Kingdom of the Crystal Skull*. We looked up at the Empire State Building, majestically needling heaven, strolled down Fifth Avenue and its Aladdin caves of shopping, checked out Rockefeller Center and Radio City Music Hall, and even made our way through Broadway and the theatre district. We also spent some time in the New York Public Library, where we had already done an event, looking around the parts we had not had a chance to see before and after our performance there.

As always with the two of us, there was the need for a cup of tea to refresh us and we found a very posh restaurant that served tea in silver ware. It was expensive and Aeronwy insisted on treating me.

She, in fact, generously treated me to cups of teas and meals so often. We had some delicate cakes, and it was lovely to get inside from the frenzy of it all for a half hour or so. After our tea break, we walked and walked as the hours unfolded, and we continued to take in the intriguing delights of the city. We eventually treated ourselves to a sit down in Bryant Park, where we decided to take in the sun for a while, along with the many making the most of it.

The fine weather had brought out families, young couples, and solitary men and women. Beyond the long lawn of spring grass, there was the canyon-deep gap that divided the skyscrapers. It was so good for us to relax, time off from reading in rooms full of strangers. We gathered our own thoughts separately in the heat of Manhattan. We decided we did not fancy heading for Ground Zero or The Dakota and so we opted for going back to Penn Station and having a meal in Merrick.

We walked from Merrick Train Station to the La Piazza restaurant, where Stan had taken us. As we ate our meal, we talked about our day out and what was in front of us in two days time, when we would leave Stan, Bebe, and Casa Barkan behind and head across America by ourselves.

Out and about in Manhattan.
© 2008 Peter Thabit Jones

Bryant Park, Manhattan.
© 2008 Peter Thabit Jones

SUNDAY, APRIL 20: LONG ISLAND

Free day.

We were up and about before Stan and Bebe returned home from visiting relatives and did our usual walk to Starbucks for a cup of tea and then on to Trader Joe's. On our way back, we sat for a while on a bench by the Cammanns Pond, next to the Norman J. Levy Lakeside School, where swans and ducks waited for visitors and their food treats.

MONDAY, APRIL 21: LONG ISLAND

The authors will pack for departure on Tuesday.

We would not return to Casa Barkan until May 3rd, so we both made sure we had all we would need for our travelling and for our residing at the hotels booked for us and the homes of our hosts. Stan had already shipped batches of Aeronwy's *Burning Bridges* book and my *The Lizard Catchers* to our various hosts for the planned book signing sessions after our events. That evening we went out for a meal with Stan and Bebe. We had a very early start in the morning, so we bedded down earlier than usual.

TUESDAY, APRIL 22: MICHIGAN

9 am: Depart Northwest Airlines from JFK; 11:07 am arrive Detroit Wayne County Airport; 12:05 pm depart; 2 pm arrive Marquette County Airport, Marquette, Michigan. Picked up and taken to reception at the home of host, Professor Beverly Matherne, Ishpeming, Michigan.

The Northwest plane dropped into a slow glide. Below, patches of snow marred our first glimpse of Michigan. A grey and frozen lake stared up at the sky as we descended. The plane safely bumped and braked as it cruised along the tarmac. I took in a breath like a sigh. We were at our latest destination. Our host, Professor Beverly Matherne, welcomed us and she drove us to a place where we could have a refreshing cup of tea and a chat, before driving us to her home. She presented us with a specially made cake that announced "Welcome Aeronwy and Peter". We were both very touched by the gesture of kindness.

Beverly's large, elegant white wooden home turned out, as she told us, to be the historic Butler House in Ishpeming, Michigan. Aeronwy and I were very impressed by the vintage furniture in every room, including a wooden rocking chair, and by the fact that we both had a four-poster bed for our stay with Beverly. After placing our luggage in our respective rooms, we sat and had tea and biscuits.

Beverly had organized a welcoming reception party of fifty guests, including some of her colleagues and students, and the evening went well as Aeronwy and I chatted with people about her father, his poetry and our poetry. One of those we talked with was the poet Russell Thorburn, whose work I eventually published in my magazine.

After the party guests had left, Beverly mischievously invited Aeronwy and me to climb a ladder to the attic, as she told us it was haunted by a ghost. I took up the challenge and stepped up each rung, as safe a heartbeat, as Aeronwy and Beverly, both smiling, urged me on. As I lifted the attic door, I gasped in a stopped moment, my body chilled, as I saw a stilled vintage chair that was waiting to rock. Down below, Aeronwy and Beverly could hardly contain their loud laughter.

Just arrived in North Michigan.
© 2008 Peter Thabit Jones

The lovely cake for us from Beverly Matherne.
© 2008 Peter Thabit Jones

WEDNESDAY, APRIL 23: MICHIGAN

11 am: Interview on local NPR station.

We were up early for an interview with the North Michigan University Public Broadcasting station. The interview brought out some of Aeronwy's memories of her father and The Boathouse in Laugharne, which were beautifully captured at the time in her book *A Daughter Remembers Dylan: Christmas and Other Memories*, published by Merton Books, and her thoughts about his fame in America. I spoke about his craftsmanship as a poet and my beginnings as a young poet in Eastside Swansea. We also talked about our tour and our own poetry. We were both at ease with such interviews, be they radio or with newspaper journalists. Aeronwy usually said to me after an interview and an event, "That went well. What do you think?"

North Michigan University Public Broadcasting.
© 2008 Peter Thabit Jones

7 pm: Reading at the Women's Federated Clubhouse, Marquette. Hosts: Beverly Matherne, poet, Professor of English, Former Director of Master of Fine Arts in Creative Writing in English and Stephanie McKenzie, poet, Assistant Professor of English, MFA Reading Series Coordinator. This program sponsored by the MFA program in Creative in the English Department at NMU and *Passages North* **literary magazine.**

We faced around a hundred people in the large room at the Women's Federated Clubhouse on 104 West Ridge Street, Marquette. We had already met some of them at Beverly's welcoming party for us. Aeronwy and I were ready to enjoy ourselves and present works that would reward those who had come to see us. We read our work and Dylan's to an audience in tune with what we were offering. Our sections from *Under Milk Wood* were particularly appreciated. We felt we managed to bring the audience into parts of that mythical Welsh place called Llaregyb and for them to experience some of the eccentric characters that inhabited it, thanks to Dylan's very mischievous and carefully plotted humour.

We talked with some of Beverly's students and colleagues about our own individual approaches to poetry, and we continued the vibrant discussions during a dinner at the very grand Landmark Hotel. Once again, we had landed in an American state and provided our programme to an audience; and, once again, we would leave the state as quickly as we had arrived. Both of us were beginning to understand a little bit of how Aeronwy's father must have felt when crossing America. We, though, had each other for support. He had done it all alone and on a far larger scale, with his legendary fame always burning at his feet.

Beverly drove us to the airport the next day and after our cheerful farewells, we were ready to fulfill another aspect of our schedule.

BEVERLY MATHERNE

During the Dylan Thomas Tribute Tour of America, orchestrated by Stanley Barkan at Cross-Cultural Communications (CCC) in 2008, I was delighted to highlight Aeronwy Thomas and Peter Thabit Jones as featured poets in our MFA Reading Series, of which I was director at the time.

They arrived on April 21, to a reception of 50 guests at my home, the historic Butler House, in Ishpeming, Michigan. Enchanted by the Queen Anne Victorian, replete with bay windows, wraparound porch, and antique furnishings, Aeronwy and Peter were delighted and comfortable.

The following day, they presented an unforgettable program at the Women's Federated Clubhouse in Marquette, the lovely Victorian venue we chose for them because of its huge parlor capable of accommodating the almost 100 people who attended. Aeronwy read and discussed her own poetry in *Burning Bridges*, her latest title from CCC, and also presented favorites of her father's poetry. Peter lectured on Dylan and read from his new book from CCC, *The Lizard Catchers*. The work of both poets was quite well taken, judging from the hearty applause each received, but what unglued the audience was the final offering that evening, a performance from *Under Milk Wood*, the two comporting themselves like professional actors, their diction professional, their timing perfect. They dazzled, we laughed, our rib cages sore when it ended.

Aeronwy and Peter spoke at length with our graduate students, taking note of their hopes and interests and e-mails, at both the earlier welcome reception at my home and, after their presentation, the cocktail-and-dinner afterglow at the Landmark Inn, Marquette's most prominent hotel. They made our students feel special, fueling their desire to please an audience equally well someday with their own poetry.

I first met Aeronwy and Peter in May of 2007, when Tino Villaneuva and I were invited as American poets to read together at the Dylan Thomas Centre in Swansea, an event arranged by Stanley at CCC and sponsored by Peter's *The Seventh Quarry Magazine*. Tino and I become fast friends and got to know many lovely people in and around Swansea, including Aeronwy and Peter. Later, Peter took us on unforgettable tours in and around the city. Dear to my heart still are the farm that inspired Dylan's great poem, "Fern Hill"; the Cliff Walk, Dylan's writing shed, and the Boathouse at Laugharne; the Victorian home where Dylan grew up, at 5 Cwmdonkin, in Swansea; St. Martin's Church, where Dylan and Caitlin are buried; and various pubs about town. We were all reunited one last time at the International Poetry Festival organized by CCC and held in Swansea from June 15-18, 2011. Once again, I heard birds keen in that characteristic way they do there and watched billyduckers dive at Laugharne.

Beverly Matherne.
© 2008 Beverly Matherne

THURSDAY, APRIL 24: ILLINOIS

2.35 pm: Depart Mesaba Aviation/NWA Airlink, Marquette County Airport; 4.20 pm arrive Detroit Wayne County Airport; 5.07 pm depart; 5.30 pm arrive Moline Quad-City Airport, Miline, Illinois. Picked up and taken to Knox College, Galesburg, Illinois. Hosted by Professor and poet Robin Metz, Program in Creative Writing, Department of English. The poets' accommodations at local motel.

We arrived at Moline Quad-City Airport, both slightly tired but ready for the next stage of the tour. Robin Metz, professor and poet, wearing a tweed Breton-type hat and a faded denim coat and light blue scarf, met us at the Arrivals area. He, along with Liz, his professor wife, had organized a busy schedule whilst we were with them in Chicago. He drove us to our motel and we talked about our tour up to that point. We booked in at the reception and took our luggage up to our rooms. Later, Robin collected us and we went to a restaurant for an evening meal. Aeronwy and I could not finish our salads, literally big bowls of lettuce etc., and so Robin asked for doggy bags and he drove us to an area where there were homeless people and passed our leftovers on to them. It was a gesture that personally endeared me to Robin.

FRIDAY, APRIL 25: ILLINOIS

Reading at Knox College, Galesburg, Illinois. Hosted by Professor Robin Metz.

Robin picked us up from our motel and drove us to Knox College. Founded in 1837, it is located at 2 E South Street, Galesburg. A coeducational private liberal arts college, Robin informed us it attracted the children of the elite across America. The college is very proud of its connections to President Abraham Lincoln, who debated the issue of slavery with Stephen A. Douglas, the fifth in a series of debates, on the site of the "Old Main" on its east side, in 1858. The college awarded Lincoln its first honorary doctorate in 1860.

We followed Robin, as both Aeronwy and I noted the glass-cased information about Lincoln on corridor walls, to the room where we would give our readings. There were about thirty students gathered to hear us read in the room that looked like the large parlour of a posh house. There was a microphone in front of the fireplace, above which was a portrait of a serious-faced Abraham Lincoln. On the ceiling directly above, there hung a fancy lit-up chandelier.

Robin introduced me and I proceeded to read my poems, making some brief comments when I felt it was necessary to set the scene for a poem. I had specifically chosen some poems from a poem-sequence I had written on slavery. I had, in fact, read the whole sequence at a 2006 exhibition on slavery, *Everywhere in Chains*, which showed the Welsh connections to slavery, at the National Waterfront Museum in Swansea. Aeronwy took her place in front of the microphone and she read powerfully. I recall Robin saying to me later how much he loved her poems *Daughter* and *Later than Laugharne*.

We mingled with the students for a while, answering their questions and listening to some of them telling us about their poetry. I invited several of them to send poems to me for consideration for my magazine, *The Seventh Quarry Swansea Poetry Magazine*. The event over, Robin took us up to see his professor's room on another level of the building. I remember his academic gown and cap hung on a clothes hanger on one of the walls.

Knox College, Galesburg, Illinois.
© 2008 Peter Thabit Jones

The microphone waits for Aeronwy and me at Knox College.
© 2008 Peter Thabit Jones

SATURDAY, APRIL 26: CHICAGO

7 pm: Reading at Chicago Poetry Society, Green Mill Jazz Club. Co-hosted by Professor Robin Metz and Professor Elizabeth Carlin-Metz.

We arrived at the Green Mill Jazz Club, with its green neon light ablaze in the spring evening, not knowing what to expect. We were to be the Special Guests at the Uptown Poetry Slam. Both of us had never been to a poetry slam, never mind participate in one. The very words, poetry slam, conjured up images in my mind of poetry rappers, those more concerned with the poem on the stage than the poem on the page.

Situated in the Uptown neighbourhood of Chicago, at 4802 N Broadway Street, Illinois, it is a venue rich in history. Frank Sinatra and Charlie Chaplin frequented the Club, and the mobster leader Al

Capone made it a speakeasy for the mobsters of the city. Founded by poet Marc Smith, the Uptown Poetry Slam at the Club was the first poetry slam in the world, though it was originally launched at the Get Me High Lounge.

Robin introduced us to Marc and then we sat at a table in a booth in the impressive décor of the lounge and watched as each poetry slammer took to the stage and stood before the microphone. Behind them was an unlit Green Mill sign. There was a terrific atmosphere in the packed room, the audience seated at tables and at the bar. We were actually surprised by the poets performing before us. They represented a variety of styles and subject matter. Earlier, at breakfast, Aeronwy and I had discussed our choice of poems for the unusual, for us, event. We both decided we would stick with our usual choices with regard to our own poems, and still include some Dylan poems.

It was then our time to be introduced and to take our turns in entertaining the animated crowd in front of us. I read my poems and I finished with Dylan's *Do not go gentle into that good night*. Aeronwy smiled at me as I left the stage and she then read her delicate, controlled, and highly effective poems. She finished with her father's tour-de-force *And death shall have no dominion*. The reaction to our readings was wild applause, with some in the audience wolf-whistling and cheering.

It was a great experience to be a part of a regular and obviously very popular poetry event. We had much to chat about when Robin drove us to a restaurant for a celebratory meal.

When we had some leisure time, Robin took us to the Carl Sandburg Birthplace, a three-room cottage, which is now a museum dedicated to the American poet and folk-singer, on E Third Street in Galesburg. The Birthplace was fascinating, with the minimal living-quarters, and the museum with its walls and glass cases of photos and information. They even had his guitar on display. Then Robin, Aeronwy, and I went out into the Quotation Walk in the garden area, where pale paving stones bear quotations from some of Sandburg's poems. Then we stopped at the Remembrance Rock, where Sandburg and his wife Lilian are laid to rest.

Marc Smith, poet and founder of the poetry slam, at the Green Mill Jazz Club event.
© 2008 Peter Thabit Jones

Carl Sandburg Birthplace, Galesburg, Illinois.
© 2008 Peter Thabit Jones

With the caretaker of the Carl Sandburg Birthplace.
© 2008 Peter Thabit Jones

Robin and Aeronwy at the Carl Sandburg Birthplace.
© 2008 Peter Thabit Jones

SUNDAY, APRIL 27: CHICAGO

Recording for e.poets with Kurt Heintz at Vitalist Theatre Company, Chicago, Illinois.
Reading at Vitalist Theatre Company, Chicago, Illinois. Co-hosted by theatre co-founders Professor Robin Metz, Executive Producer/Contributing Artist, and Professor Elizabeth Carlin Metz, Artistic Director.

The Vitalist Theatre Company, founded in 1997 by Robin and Liz, is based at Theatre Building Chicago, which is on West Belmont Avenue in the city's Lakeview neighborhood. A wonderful production of *A Passage to India*, directed by Liz, was taking place when Aeronwy and I were with Robin and we attended a performance on the night before our readings at the Theatre. We both thoroughly enjoyed dramatist Martin Sherman's colourful adaptation of E. M. Forster's novel.

In the afternoon of our evening readings, Robin took us to the theatre for us to be recorded by Kurt Heintz, the Chicago founder and publisher of e.poets.net. Kurt, a really nice guy, told us all about e.poets and informed us that our audio contributions would be available on-line. He then proceeded to record us reading some of our own poems on the actual set of *A Passage to India*. Both of us had already decided our choices and discussed them at breakfast in our motel. I read my poems *Rat, Ghosts, Stanzas for the Dead, Stones, Bereavement* (from a poem-sequence about the loss of my second son, Mathew), and *Bob Dylan, Cardiff, Wales*. Aeronwy read her father's *Fern Hill* and her own poems, *Moon, Sorry, Daughter, The Night Watch, The Road Home*, and *Road to Heaven*. Aeronwy and I were both very pleased to be a part of Kurt's on-line recordings of poets reading their works and we were most grateful to Robin for organizing the session.

Aeronwy and I faced another full audience for our evening readings at the theatre. Those present included members of The Chicago Tafia Welsh Society, David Parry, the Society's President, and Winston Evans and his wife, Mary Ann de la Cruz, and the actors and actresses from the production of *A Passage to India*.

I read my poems, then Dylan's *The force that through the green fuse drives the flower* and *Do not go gentle into that good night*. Then Aeronwy read her poems, some prose-pieces about her childhood, followed by her father's *Fern Hill* and *And death shall have no dominion*. We finished with sections from *Under Milk Wood*, which proved particularly popular. We stayed on the stage for the Q & A session, in which we also received some kind comments about our own poems among the keen questions about Dylan, personal and academic.

The evening concluded with Robin, Liz, Aeronwy, and I joining the Vitalist Theatre actors and actresses in a restaurant that was a short walk from the theatre building.

Theatre Building Chicago, home of the Vitalist Theatre Company.
© 2008 Peter Thabit Jones

Robin Metz in the Chicago theatre.
© 2008 Peter Thabit Jones

With members of the Chicago Tafia Welsh Society: Winston Evans with his wife, Mary Ann, and David Parry, the President of the Society.
© 2008 Peter Thabit Jones

MONDAY, APRIL 28: IOWA

Reading at Iowa International Writers Workshop, University of Iowa.

We had almost a two-hour drive from Galesburg to the University of Iowa, where we would read at the Iowa International Writers Workshop at 7 pm in the Shambaugh House, the home of the Writers Programme. It was an exciting prospect to be reading at this prestigious venue, and our event was part of National Poetry Month being celebrated at the University. Robin, in fact, was an M.F.A. graduate of the Writers Workshop at the University of Iowa, and we listened to his stories about being a student there.

The drive was relaxing and visually stunning. We drove through a landscape as flat as the surface of a table and a view that seemed to go on forever on both sides of the road. The ominous, grey sky looked ready to break and confront us with a downpour like a biblical warning.

We arrived at the Shambaugh House at 430 N Clinton Street well before the starting time for our event. Robin parked his car and we stretched our legs by looking around the campus. He took us to a place for coffee and we chatted among ourselves as Aeronwy and I found that required relaxing space within oneself before giving a reading.

The Shambaugh House was exactly like entering someone's very comfortable home. American poet and teacher Paul Engle founded the International Writing Programme in 1967, and famous writers such as Rita Dove, Flannery O'Connor, Robert Bly, and Jorie Graham had connections with it, so we were stepping into a very special place. A black and white portrait photo of Paul Engle dominated the wall above the wooden fireplace, which had two shaded and lit-up lamps on the mantlepiece. The microphone and the wooden lectern set up for Aerowny and me were in front of the fireplace.

Christopher Merrill, poet and director of the International Writers Programme, introduced us to a packed room. As we presented our readings, an audio recording was made of the event. The Q & A session was enjoyable, and we left yet another event with the feeling we had connected with people who would hopefully return to Dylan's works and maybe seek out more of our works.

We both liked Robin very much and having been a part of so many events with him, there was a touch of sadness in our farewells at the Moline Quad-City Airport the following morning for our flight to our next stop: Boulder, Colorado.

Robin would, though, come to Wales several times for events organised by me, including one in conjunction with him and Liz and Knox College when I guided them and a large group of their students around places in Wales associated with Dylan Thomas in 2010. The visit was part of a 12-week seminar, Dylan Thomas in Wales, being offered by Robin at Knox College. Robin also accompanied me to Satu Mare in Romania when he and I gave readings and talks at colleges and venues, even appearing on Romanian television. The visit was organised by my Romanian translator, Dr. Olimpia Iacob in 2009. Robin, a very dear friend of mine, passed away in November 2018.

The portrait of American poet Paul Engle in the Shambaugh House.
© 2008 Peter Thabit Jones

TUESDAY, APRIL 29: COLORADO

**1.52 pm Depart United Express/Tran States from Moline Quad-City Airport; 3.05 pm arrive Denver International Airport, Denver, Colorado. Picked up and taken to home of Professor Paul M. Levitt, host.
7.30 pm: Reading, followed by Q&A session at University of Colorado, JILA Auditorium, Boulder, Colorado. Accommodations at the home of Professor Paul Levitt.**

Professor and eminent novelist Paul M. Levitt, tall and smiling, was waiting for us behind a barrier as Aeronwy and I acclimatized ourselves mentally and physically after another flight and the official ritual of another airport's passengers' processing system. He led us to a carpark and we slowly made our way out of the airport and into a very warm and clear day. Boulder is a city at the foothills of the Rocky Mountains, twenty-five miles from Denver; and the leisurely drive there provided us with beautiful scenery. The Flatirons, craggy rock formations, dramatically overlook the sprawl of the city.

We left our luggage at Paul's home, where we were introduced to his charming wife, Nancy, and then Paul took us on the short walk to the University of Colorado Boulder, which is known for being the home of the main campus of the University of Colorado, the state's largest university. He pointed out various parts of the campus as we made our way to the top floor of the Physics Department building, which gave us a spectacular view of the Flatirons breaching the evening sky. A group of professors and students had turned up for our reading, and so Aeronwy and I decided to just sit down among them and deliver our poems. It was probably the most relaxed reading we gave during the whole tour. Even in such a small and friendly gathering, Aeronwy had a charismatic presence. After we read, Paul said that *Fern Hill* was a favourite poem of his, and during the Q & A session, a physics professor complimented me on my poem *Stones*. He said he had had a lifelong love of stones, and he wanted to know how he could get a copy of my poem, which was not included in my *The Lizard Catchers* book. It was a lovely start to our time in Boulder.

A view of part of the University of Boulder Campus from
Paul and Nancy Levitt's home.
© 2008 Peter Thabit Jones

The view from the top of the Physics Department building.
© 2008 Peter Thabit Jones

WEDNESDAY, APRIL 30: COLORADO

7.30 pm: Reading, followed by Q&A and book signing at the Boulder Public Library Canyon Theater, Boulder. Hosted by Professor Paul M. Levitt.

On the morning of our reading at Boulder Public Library Canyon Theater, Nancy, Paul's wife, took Aeronwy and me into Boulder's shopping center. She needed to get some things for the meal she planned to cook for us after our evening event. We walked from their home along the length of a river. It was a hot afternoon and young students jogged and bicycled past us. One girl sat on a rock, smoothing her big dog and fingering the quick swirl of flowing water. We reached a supermarket store, with the breathtaking backdrop of the range of Flatiron mountains reigning over Boulder. After a tea with Nancy in the store, she made her way back home whilst Aeronwy and I decided to check out other parts of the shopping center.

We walked along busy Pearl Street Mall, enjoying the exercise and noting the many statues placed in various parts of the pedestrian zone, including a large statue of an imposing buffalo and a large elk. We grabbed a coffee at a local cafeteria and discussed the evening's event. We both liked Boulder and its laidback atmosphere very much. We headed back, Aeronwy to Paul's friends' home and I to Paul's and Nancy's home, to relax and to prepare for our event.

Boulder Public Library is a two-storey building and the Canyon Theater is a splendid venue for public performances. We had attracted a large crowd, thanks to Paul's promotional work before we arrived in Boulder. Once again, after introductions we took to a stage, to offer our words to unknown faces, to try to startle the moments with our measured workings of truths, and to give parts of our lives for the rewards of scattering applause. After the readings, people gathered around us as we sat at a table displaying our books for purchase and to ask us more questions. We received excellent feedback from those who spoke to us about our event and Paul also introduced us to some of his friends, who were equally enthusiastic about our readings.

Our time with Paul and Nancy was most enjoyable. They were kind and gracious hosts. We said our goodbyes and Paul generously invited us back to Boulder. I did return the following year, to be on various panels at the World Conference Affairs and I returned twice again at Paul's invitation. Aeronwy did not, but I know she treasured our times in Boulder, both of us taken in by the magnificent landscape and the seemingly slow pace of everything. One of Paul's students, Sarah, drove us to Denver Airport and we sat waiting for our flight, sipping tea and discussing our tour up to that point. We were headed for California, the penultimate event of our tour, before returning to New York.

PAUL M. LEVITT

When Stanley Barkan, the publisher of *CCC Poetry*, telephoned and asked if I could arrange a reading for Peter and Aeronwy, in Boulder, Colorado, where I was teaching, I quickly agreed. Boulder was to be just one stop on their American tour. Having some familiarity with Peter's poetry and an abiding affection for Dylan Thomas, I knew I was in for a treat. The only question was: how to arrange suitable occasions for the events. Most academic calendars are full by the start of the fall semester, so I knew that my home department, English, would be already committed to numerous events. But the right campus opportunity presented itself when I heard that the chairman of Physics, John Cumalat, was retiring from that office, though not from the department. He is a man I greatly admire for his administrative and scholarly accomplishments. The Physics Department has its own auditorium, with steeply raked seating. I reserved that space and told John that I wanted to celebrate his many successful years in office.

I then approached the Boulder Public Library, which has a comfortable space (the Canyon Theatre) for concerts, readings, movies, and lectures. The library director enthusiastically welcomed the idea of a reading and suggested that a table be placed outside the theatre to display Peter's and Aeronwy's books. After the reading, the two of them could then retire to the table for sales and signing.

Although my wife and I invited both Peter and Aeronwy to stay with us at our Boulder house, which is located across the street from the campus, on Hillside Road, Aeronwy accepted the invitation of a friend of mine to stay nearby. Peter moved into our second-floor guest room and almost immediately disappeared to compose, so devoted was he to his writing. If I ran a B&B, I couldn't have asked for a better lodger than Peter: discreet, quiet, undemanding, and a source of innumerable stories and tales. If, as Samuel Johnson observed, the height of civilization is good food and conversation, we were enjoying a golden interlude. My wife provided wonderful repasts, and Peter provided spellbinding talk.

The curtain came up on Tuesday, April 29. Flying from Moline, Illinois to Denver, Colorado, my two guests arrived in the afternoon (3:05) at Denver International Airport (DIA), in Denver, Colorado. The escalator brought them up from the train, which connects to the different terminals. Standing behind a barrier, I wore a red sweater to identify myself. We collected luggage, went to the car park, and drove to Boulder, a trip of about 50 minutes. We didn't have a great deal of time to spare, since the reading in the physics building (to be precise, the JILA Auditorium) was scheduled for 7:30 pm. Around 7:00, we left my house and crossed the street to the campus, passing Macky Auditorium, the library, the buildings housing MCDB and psychology. As the time for the reading was nearly upon us, I saw that the attendance was small enough to hold the reading in the jewel of the Physics building, the top floor, which has picture windows on three sides that look out to the mountains on the western slope and to the football stadium across the street. The lights of the city could easily be seen glittering in the darkness. We retired to couches and lounge chairs and sat back to listen to Peter and Aeronwy. After the reading, the guests asked questions and seemed delighted to come away with some signed books.

On Wednesday April 30, we drove to the public library, which is situated on Boulder Creek (a river, really), where we were met by a wonderfully receptive crowd. Among the guests was a retired colleague of mine who, like me, wanted to hear about Dylan Thomas. In fact,

Aeronwy asked if we would like to hear a particular poem of her father's, and we replied, "Fern Hill." As she recited it, I found myself repeating the words and feeling emotionally moved. Both Peter and Aeronwy read from their own works and, afterwards, answered questions and signed books. Many of the guests huddled in the lobby, circling the table, wanting to ask further questions and come to know the poets personally. Numerous friends stopped me to express their thanks for a splendid evening, and wanted to know when our poets might be returning. Alas, although Peter did, Aeronwy did not. We returned to my house for dinner and more talk. Later, they left me with a canvas satchel of extra copies of their books for distribution to interested parties, a lovely gesture.

The next day, May 1, my friends, which indeed they had become, left for the airport. After they had left, I felt a hole in my life that hadn't been there before, and swore to read more poetry and begin dinners with my teenage grandchildren by reading a poem, often one by Peter or Aeronwy.

I have little to no sense of how my guests felt about finding themselves in the Rocky Mountains, reading lines lifted from their lives. Although they thanked me profusely for hosting the events and seeing to their housing and meals, I occasionally ask myself whether they felt the cultural differences that I often felt when my father immersed me in tales of snowy Russia.

Paul M. Levitt.
© 2019 Paul M. Levitt

THURSDAY, MAY 1: CALIFORNIA

11:15 am Depart United Airlines Denver International Airport; 12:48 pm arrive San Jose Municipal Airport, San Jose, California. Picked up and taken to motel in Carmel by John Dotson, poet/ Senior Editor at McGraw-Hill. Evening welcome. Hosted by John Dotson and Friends of C. G. Jung.

John Dotson, a prodigious writer and, as we learned later, superb sculptor, was waiting for us as we once more went through an airport's arrival procedures. We were in California, again following in the footsteps of her iconic father. John was very pleasant and enthusiastic and, despite our tiredness as the tour and travelling were beginning to take their toll, we listened with much interest to his plans for us whilst residing in Carmel. He emphasised there were no demands and that we would have time to relax and enjoy Carmel whilst with him.

We listened, as he drove us from the airport, about his longtime interest in Dylan Thomas and of Dylan's two visits to this part of America, which we both knew about, but John's full knowledge of poet and dramatist Robinson Jeffers (he has written a book about residing at Jeffers' Tor House) and of novelist Henry Miller added much colour to Dylan's connections to the area.

John had arranged for us to be interviewed at McGowan House in Monterey by a reporter from the *Monterey Herald*. McGowan House, which serves as the parish hall for Saint James Episcopal Church, is a special place, a centre for good causes and intellectual events. Laith Agha, the reporter arrived in the parking area at the same time as we. We answered his questions, with Aeronwy at one point saying about our tour, "I'm hoping one of the byproducts is that more people will go back and read his poetry". We had our photo taken for the article and then it was time to meet some of the people connected with McGowan House, including the elderly Joe Pagano, whose very kind spirit endeared him to us.

Whilst in Carmel-By-The-Sea and thanks to John's kindness, we were going to stay at The Homestead, owned by legendary film star Clint Eastwood. I was given the key to room 45 and Aeronwy had the key to room 51. Our rooms, in fact, were more like wooden cabins within the wooden lodging complex and we were very pleased. Joyce, the receptionist, had worked for Clint Eastwood for decades and we gave her signed copies of our books, *Burning Bridges* and *The Lizard Catchers*, as she was very interested in why we were in Carmel-By-The-Sea.

We had time to stroll around the small city before John planned to pick us up and take us to Big Sur, for an evening meal at Nepenthe Restaurant on Highway One. We came upon the Tuck Box restaurant, a 1927 cottage, like something out of a fairytale, on Dolores Street. It was there that we both agreed we had found the best cup of tea during our time in America. We sat and talked as we enjoyed some jam and scones. We agreed to have breakfast there in the morning. We then went for a walk, around a place that is full of charm and fascinating shops to browse around.

John picked us up in his car and he drove us out of Carmel-By-The-Sea and towards Big Sur, where we headed for Nepenthe Restaurant. We took in some of the truly stunning and visually dramatic landscape on the way, the rugged coast and the wild and ever-restless Pacific Ocean. John told us about Big Sur and its importance to writers such as Lawrence Ferlinghetti, who had a cabin in Bixby Canyon. Jack Kerouac stayed at the cabin and the result was his novel *Big Sur*. Nepenthe, which is lodged on top of a peak of the Santa Lucia Mountains, has been a calling-pace for artists, poets, writers, bohemians and celebrities down the decades.

Dylan and Caitlin had spent time at Nepenthe when they were in California in 1952, and so it was rather special to be there with Aeronwy as we ate, drank and enjoyed the evening, whilst John told us about some of the famous people who frequented the restaurant. I did not know then, even though I took a photo of the weather-worn Phoenix Bird wooden sculpture on the patio of Nepenthe, that three years later I would begin to write a drama about its creator, Big Sur reclusive sculptor, Edmund Kara.

On the way back to The Homestead, Aeronwy fell asleep in the car as John and I discussed all kinds of things. It was something we would do many times on my return to Big Sur as a writer-in-residence there over nine summers. That, though, was all in the future.

FRIDAY, MAY 2: CALIFORNIA

Luncheon at Tor House, home of famous American poet Robinson Jeffers.
7 pm: Monterey Peninsula College. Coordinated by Elliott Ruchowitz-Roberts, Vice President, Robinson Jeffers Tor House Foundation, with Charlotte Rose, President, Monterey Peninsula Friends of C. G. Jung, and Phyllis Sears, Treasurer of President of Monterey Peninsula Friends of C. G. Jung.
Program: John Dotson, Director, Monterey Peninsula Friends of C. G. Jung, Robin Robinson, Director, Monterey Peninsula Friends of C. G. Jung, Phyllis Sears, Treasurer, Monterey Peninsula Friends of C. G. Jung
Introduction: host John Dotson
Peter Thabit Jones: Craftsmanship of Dylan Thomas
Aeronwy Thomas: Memories
Aeronwy Thomas: Poetry of Dylan Thomas
Peter Thabit Jones: His own poetry from *The Lizard Catchers*, **et al.**
Aeronwy Thomas: Her own poetry from *Burning Bridges*, **et al.**
Presented by The Robinson Jeffers Tor House Foundation, Monterey Peninsula Friends of C. G. and Monterey College, Monterey, California.

John picked us up at The Homestead, and we headed for the bay area of Carmel-By-The-Sea, where the Robinson Jeffers Tor House is situated. Once there, we were introduced to Elliott Ruchowitz-Roberts, the Vice President of the Robinson Jeffers Tor House Foundation, Taelen Thomas, a local actor known for performing the works of Dylan Thomas, and Joe Pagano from McGowan House.

It was great to see a poster advertising our evening event at the Monterey Peninsula College on the open door of the Tor House gift shop.

One cannot describe the feeling of seeing Tor House, in fact two structures, Tor House and Hawk Tower. Hawk Tower is an artwork of rocks, crafted slowly and carefully, and it stands magnificently like the remains of a castle. As with Carl Sandburg's Birthplace home in Galesburg, Illinois, and Walt Whitman's Birthplace in West Hills, New York, it was such a rewarding experience to be shown around such an important literary place. I, with some other visitors there, went up to the top of Hawk Tower, whilst Aeronwy sat on a bench below with Joe and Taelen.

After luncheon, John drove us to Point Lobos State Natural Reserve, a coastal area of outstanding scenery. As we left the car and made our way along a marked trail, he warned us about poison oak, a three-leaved shrub that can give one an extremely unpleasant rash if one makes contact with it. We walked at a leisurely pace until we reached the torn coast with sandy beaches, where seals lolled around like victims of a battle, and the eternal machine of the ocean busied itself. After the American tour, Aeronwy and I would both respond to the sacred haven of Point Lobos and memorialize our visit with a poem. John returned us to The Homestead, so that we could rest and get ready for our evening performance.

Our event in the Lecture Forum at Monterey Peninsula College, which is situated on Freemont Street, had attracted a large crowd. For the final time on the tour, we took to a stage. John introduced us and I started the evening by speaking about the craftsmanship in some of Dylan's poems and his use of Welsh-language devices. I used a projector to illustrate aspects of my talk. Aeronwy followed me and she gave a wonderful speech about the memories of her life in the Thomas family. It was my turn again and I read from my books and then Aeronwy read from her books. We concluded the evening with our sections from *Under Milk Wood*. The audience's ripples of applause made it a successful conclusion to our final presentation in front of people who had paid to see us. We signed books and chatted with people who came up to us.

Carolyn Mary Kleefeld, an acclaimed poet and artist, and her partner at the time, David Wayne Dunn, also a poet and artist, came to speak to me, and they gave me a copy of their collaborative book, *Kissing Darkness*. I did not know then how important Carolyn would be to my writing career. She would, in fact, invite me to be a writer-in-residence in Big Sur in her cabin for nine summers, starting in 2010.

John would also become a very dear friend, and we would share a lot of fun times and intense discussions about Dylan Thomas during my residencies when I spent my breaks from the cabin with him and his friends in Carmel-By-The-Sea.

Joyce at The Homestead, with the signed books we gave her.
© 2008 Peter Thabit Jones

Charlotte Rose, Peter and Aeronwy, Joe Pagano,
photographer Robin V. Robinson, John Dotson.
© 2008 Peter Thabit Jones

Aeronwy and John at the Robinson Jeffers Tor House.
© 2008 Peter Thabit Jones

Peter at Robinson Jeffers Tor House.
© 2008 Peter Thabit Jones

Before our reading at Monterey Peninsula College.
© 2008 Peter Thabit Jones

John Dotson and Aeronwy at Bixby Bridge.
© 2008 Peter Thabit Jones

JOHN DOTSON

LAST STOP ON THE TOUR: CALIFORNIA

I did not know much about the legacy of Welsh poetry when I drove to San Jose Airport to greet Peter Thabit Jones and Aeronwy Thomas Ellis. What I did know, though, was very important to me, as I had learned in *The White Goddess* by Robert Graves. His theme, which I took to heart in my youth, concerns the "divinatory and prophetic gifts . . . of the original Welsh master-poets . . . and the rediscovery of the lost rudiments and active principles of poetic magic." No small matters. While such wondering was in the deep background of my wait at baggage claim that spring day in 2008, my immediate assignment was to stand at the foot of the escalator and discern the descending faces of Peter and Aeronwy.

Peter I knew only from the description by Stanley Barkan, and Aeronwy I knew only by association with her father and his work–of which I was an appreciator, teacher, and broadcaster. I was also well aware that Dylan Thomas had twice visited central California, twice met with the great California poet Robinson Jeffers, and that these facts in themselves were sufficient cause for Peter and Aeronwy to include Monterey and Big Sur on their tour. In the marrow of my bones, I felt the resonances of their mission belonged with the profound "rudiments and active principles of poetic magic" that endure *here,* "west of the west of things," as Jeffers put it.

I recognized them instantaneously, Peter and Aeronwy, as they clutched their cases looking a bit blank and travel-weary. Their California stop had few requirements, I informed them, as we traversed the freeways of the Silicon Valley. First off, we could all duly appreciate the fact that both Dylan and Caitlin Thomas had come to Monterey in the early 1950s, and that we were thus revisiting some of the westernmost scenes in the lives of both her famous parents. Secondly, Peter and Aeronwy were scheduled for a single public appearance, at Monterey Peninsula College, the event co-sponsored by Carmel poet Elliot Ruchowitz-Roberts and the Robinson Jeffers Tor House Foundation.

Thirdly, treks to Tor House, the stone house that Jeffers built in Carmel, and Point Lobos, a reserve of outstanding natural beauty, were surely spiritual obligations. And at last, we would do well to drive down Highway One to Big Sur where Dylan had shown up uninvited and unexpected at Henry Miller's door once upon a time–and was let in. Otherwise, I assured them, they should enjoy some quiet in Carmel and refresh themselves prior to flying back east for their final appearances in New York.

The performance at the college was well attended, the audience attentive and happily engaging the poetry of Peter and Aeronwy, Peter's presentation on the Welsh poetic device of *Cynghanedd*, and finally their duo-virtuoso performance of the raucous Mr-and-Mrs-Pugh-at-table segment from Dylan's play *Under Milk Wood*. The whole situation was unique, as was luminously apparent to each and all.

I think the Tor House jaunt turned out to be trying for Aeronwy–for her to engage the dwelling place and mythos of Jeffers and his family was probably a little too much to ask. The hike at Point Lobos, however, led her to write a poem (in *Shadows and Shades* [Poetry Monthly Press 2009]), that includes these lines:

Coated and mufflered
I'm waiting here
on the cliff
away from the crumbly edge

crunching needles of
Monterey fir
stripped by the winds
to a petrified marker

the end of the world
the smell of yerba buena
and wild lilac
in the undergrowth . . .

I am looking and laughing
in the salt-laden air
as I loose my footing
and the cliff disappears.

I will return to these lines momentarily.

Our drive down the coast, pausing for photos at the iconic Bixby Creek Bridge, and then winding our way southward to the legendary Nepenthe restaurant, known for its awe-inspiring views, was our reward, a culminating moment for the three of us and our California scheme. We celebrated with a bottle of good wine, good entrées, and the freedom of lively, fully relaxed conversation. I did not know at the time that Caitlin and Dylan had once sat at the bar at Nepenthe where he "drew all over the napkins," as reported by restaurant founder Bill Fassett. This event would have occurred soon after the restaurant opened.

In May 2008, of course, there was no telling that Peter and I would find further opportunities to become enduring friends and colleagues, nor that he would eventually return for annual stays at a solitary cabin "on Big Sur," facilitated by our now long-term, mutual friend Carolyn Mary Kleefeld, author and artist extraordinaire. Peter has truly established himself as poet-playwright-novelist-in-residence in this place beyond categorizing.

In November 2008, I traveled to Wales where I joined with poet Robin Metz and his wife, dramatist Elizabeth Carlin-Metz, in *The Seventh Quarry Presents,* a series organized by Peter and coordinated among US poets by Stanley Barkan. Peter led the pilgrimage to Dylan sites, and Aeronwy traveled from London to participate. Later, when I felt an impulse to write about my experiences in Swansea, Laugharne, and Gower, Aeronwy advised via email that I "go to" and follow her father's advice to "beaver it along." That I did, with her ongoing encouragements. Though she read the raw text as I wrote, she did not see the published form.[*]

Throughout her time in California and along the paths we shared in Wales, Aeronwy was very direct about her quest to correct the many misperceptions about her father. I believe she succeeded at this, soundly, in a process brought to completeness with observances throughout the UK in 2014, the centenary of Dylan's birth.

In the email threads that we shared up to the time of her death in 2009, I felt a growing sense of what Aeronwy had expressed in her California stanzas: ". . . as I loose my footing / and the cliff disappears . . ." Perhaps she meant the word "lose" rather than "loose," but I wouldn't be sure about that. Many forces were alive in our midst that day at Punta de Los Lobos Mariños. Principles of poetic magic were very present–life-changing and prophetic as they came to be.

Love For Ever Meridian: Finding Dylan Thomas in the 21st Century, Cross-Cultural Communications/The Seventh Quarry Press [2012].

John Dotson.
© 2019 John Dotson

SATURDAY, MAY 3: LONG ISLAND

10.13 am Depart United Express/Skywest from San Jose Municipal Airport; 11.35 am arrive Los Angeles International Airport, Los Angeles; 12.21 pm depart; 9 pm arrive JFK International Airport. Picked up and taken to Casa Barkan.

We relaxed before our final event the following day. We told Stan and Bebe about our travels, the events away from the East Coast, and about some of the people we had met and how lucky we were to have such kind and generous hosts. We took some exercise by taking our final walk to Starbucks in Merrick and on to Trader Joe's, although I would take the walk many times over the coming years by myself. As we talked, we knew we would return home to the UK the day after our final event. Our adventure together, reading a selection of the famous poems by her father, sections from his *Under Milk Wood* and reading selections of our own poems would be over. We both felt we had done our best and that we had worked well as a travelling duo and as a travelling trio with Trefor.

SUNDAY, MAY 4: NEW YORK

Walking tour of Dylan Thomas sites in Manhattan, ending at the White Horse Tavern for drinks. Reading of some poems by Aeronwy Thomas and Peter Thabit Jones. Dinner at French restaurant next door. Limited to 14. Hosted by Catrin Brace, Wales International Centre.

Stan, Aeronwy, and I were joined by various dignitaries, who were invited by Catrin, such as Thomas Keith, Consulting Editor for New Directions Publishing, which published Dylan's works in America, and also by Wales' *Western Mail* reporters Karen Price and Carolyn Hitt, to visit the main places connected with Dylan Thomas in Greenwich Village. A photographer from the Wales International Centre also accompanied our group. We stopped at various places such as the Minetta Tavern and St Vincent's Hospital, which was still there before its complete demolishment in 2013.

Catrin had asked Aeronwy and me to read some of Dylan's poems at some of the places where we stopped, and they included *The hand that signed the paper* and *The force that through the green fuse drives the flower*. I could see that Aeronwy was particularly moved when we reached St Vincent's Hospital, where her father had died on 9 November 1953. She did not say anything but her silence and the look on her face said it all.

Our walk finished at the White Horse Tavern, where we celebrated the legend and the genius of Dylan Thomas with a drink. Bebe and Sultan Catto, professor and poet, had also come along to the pub.

Aeronwy and I did a reading of some of our poems to our group in the back room and to some other curious drinkers who peered in from the main bar. We stood near a walled and framed poster of her father, and I remember wondering what he would have thought of his poet daughter reading her poems in his favourite place in Greenwich Village.

We then headed next door to a French restaurant for a meal. David Slivka, a sculptor and close New York friend of Dylan's, who made the death mask of Dylan, assisted by artist Ibram Lassaw, was there and we greeted each other warmly. I first met David in 1997, when I did a ten day poetry reading tour of New York and New Jersey. The organiser of my readings, Patricia Hochron, had arranged for her and me to visit David's Hell's Kitchen studio and for me to ask him some questions for a commission I had received from Rian Evans, who was the Arts Editor of the *Western Mail* at the time, to write some Postcards from New York, to be published in the newspaper. Rian, in fact, is the daughter of another Swansea poet, John Ormond who was a friend of Dylan's and made a film, *A Bronze Mask*, about Dylan in 1968.

Adjacent to the theatre district and with a history of being the home for actors and arts associations, David's studio in Hell's Kitchen was a visual treat. He was very kind to us and he explained some of his wooden sculptures before we sat down, and I asked him various questions as we drank cups of coffee. Before I left, he gave me an original photo of the death mask of Dylan Thomas, which was taken during its actual making and a copy of an article about him and his sculptures.

Whilst Aeronwy, Stan, and I sat at our table with David and his partner Joan Ullman, enjoying our meals, Catrin came up to us and asked Aeronwy and me to research and write the first-ever official Dylan Thomas Walking Tour of Greenwich Village for the Welsh Government in New York. We would receive a payment for doing it. We were both really happy to receive such a thrilling commission, and it was a wonderful way to end our tour in honour of her father.

The written Tour originally appeared as a downloadable pdf, followed by a MP3 version, narrated by well-known Welsh actor John Pierce Jones. Then New York Fun Tours started offering a guided version, and in 2014 the book version and the smartphone app version, narrated by another well-known Welsh actor, Nicholas McGaughey, became available.

St Vincent's Hospital in 2008.
© 2008 Peter Thabit Jones

White Horse Tavern in 2008.
© 2008 Peter Thabit Jones

The book version of the Dylan Thomas Walking Tour
of Greenwich Village, published in 2014 for the
Dylan Thomas Centenary.
© 2008 Peter Thabit Jones

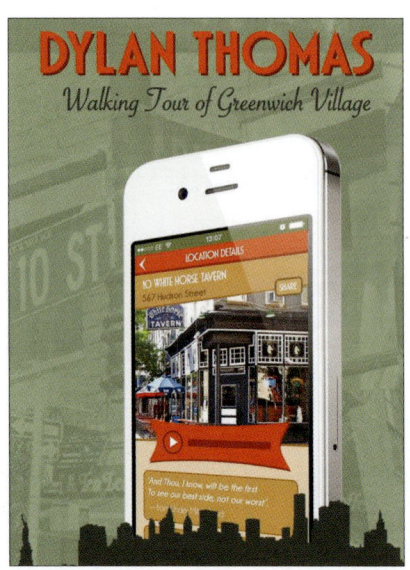

The smartphone app version of the Dylan Thomas Walking Tour of Greenwich Village, released in 2014 for the Dylan Thomas Centenary.
© 2008 Peter Thabit Jones

The New York launch of the *Dylan Thomas Walking Tour of Greenwich Village* book at the Poets House in 2014: Dylan Thomas Centenary.
© 2014 Bill Wolak

MONDAY, MAY 5: RETURN HOME

Poets return to Great Britain.

On our flight from JFK International Airport to Heathrow Airport in London, we had much to chat about in between our individual snatches of sleep. We spoke about the many highlights of our time in America and laughed at our need for a cup of tea whenever we could get one. We both thought it strange that it had come to an end and we would go our separate ways once we landed, though we knew we would meet again in Swansea at some point when Aeronwy attended an event connected with her father's work and legacy.

As we waited for Trefor to pick up Aeronwy at the Arrivals area, we grabbed a cup of tea. She asked me how I felt now that it was all over. "Sad," I said. She smiled at my reply. Trefor greeted us and I said goodbye to them. They headed to the car-park for their journey back to Surrey and I headed to the Central Bus Station, where I would get my National Express bus back to Swansea, a roughly four-and-a-half hour journey.

POSTSCRIPT

I saw Aeronwy twice more that year, both times at the Dylan Thomas Centre. The first time was mid-year when she was involved in something to do with the International Dylan Thomas Prize, thus her reason for coming to Swansea. The second time was in November when she and I gave a talk about our time in America and we read some of our poems written during our tour at the annual Dylan Thomas Festival. It was to be the last time I took to a stage with her. We did keep in touch regularly with regard to our commissioned *Dylan Thomas Walking Tour of Greenwich Village* project. She had told me to do the basic groundwork and we discussed via letters and emails aspects of its contents. We were very proud of what we were working on.

Aeronwy passed away in July 2009, far too sudden for her beloved family and far too sudden for all those whose lives she touched so magically in the UK, Europe, and America. I drove from Swansea to Surrey, to attend the funeral service in a church with her family and many friends.

I have since returned many times to America, to some of the places we visited, such as New York, Colorado, and Massachusetts, as a visiting poet doing readings, talks, and for festivals and conference panels; and I have been writer-in-residence in Big Sur, California, each summer since 2010, a place that so endeared itself to Aeronwy and me. I always think of her when I am in America and that tour of incredible experiences we shared, the laughter, the panic because of a problem, the many one-to-one chats whilst travelling or having a meal, our need for a nice cup of tea, and the sharing of her iconic father's remarkable works and our own poems to audiences across America. I miss her friendship, deeply. She was a very dear 'comrade' during our time on the tour.

I last saw Trefor in the Browns Hotel in Laugharne in April 2018. We met so that I could pass on a batch of a book that I had published by one of Aeronwy's closest friends, Frances White, who needed extra copies. Trefor was in Laugharne with his daughter Hannah and her family, and he kindly offered to take the batch of books back to England with him, which saved me the hassle of posting them. We had a lovely chat, and he, as always, was great company, warm and full of fascinating stories about Aeronwy and his father-in-law, Dylan Thomas.

The official tour photo.
© 2008 Martin Holroyd

A poster from the tour.
© 2008 Peter Thabit Jones

A poster from the tour.
© 2008 Peter Thabit Jones

Peter at the Boathouse in Laugharne, April 2017.
© 2017 Robin V. Robinson

BIOS OF THE TOUR HOSTS WHO CONTRIBUTED TO THIS BOOK

Laura Boss is a first-place winner of the Poetry Society of America's Gordon Barber Poetry Contest. Founder and editor of *Lips,* she was the sole representative of the USA at the XXVI Annual Struga Poetry Evenings in Macedonia. Her awards for her poetry also include three Poetry Fellowships from the NJSCA. Her seven books of poetry include the ALTA winning *On the Edge of the Hudson* (Cross-Cultural Communications) and, most recently, *The Best Lover (NYQ).* In 2011, she received the first International Poetry Award at the International Poetry Festival in Swansea, Wales (sponsored by CCC and The Seventh Quarry). Her poems have appeared in *The New York Times.*

Catrin Brace was born in Aberystwyth and brought up in the Vale of Glamorgan. She graduated in Welsh from Bangor University and in French from Poitiers University. Her career has spanned several years in tourism both in the Wales Tourist Board in Cardiff and in the private sector in New York. She was Head of Advertising and Sponsorship Sales for the Welsh broadcaster S4C for ten years, returning to New York in 2001 where she subsequently represented the Welsh Government for fifteen years before returning to Wales in 2017.

Kristine Doll (Boston, MA, USA) is the author of the poetry collection *Speak to Me Again* (Feral Press, 2014). "My Friends" from this book was nominated for the Pushcart Prize in Poetry. Doll is also a translator (Catalan, English, Spanish). Doll's translations and her own poetry have been published internationally in such venues as *Lyrikline* (Spain*), Confesiuni* (Romania), *The Seventh Quarry* (Wales), *Cross-Cultural Communications Art & Poetry Series Broadsides* (USA), *The Paterson*

Literary Review (USA), *Immagine i Poesia* (Italy) and *Double Dialogues* (Australia).

John Dotson is an American writer, sculptor, performer, and producer. His book *The Enduring Voice, A Tor House Journal* (1987) details his experience as poet-in-residence of the Robinson Jeffers Tor House Foundation in Carmel. His newest book, *Singing in My Chains: Hearing Dylan Thomas at the Birth of an Age* is forthcoming from Cross-Cultural Communications/The Seventh Quarry Press, New York & Wales. He is president of the Monterey Friends of CG Jung and an active participant in the International Jean Gebser Society.

Maria Mazziotti Gillan is winner of the 2014 George Garrett Award for Outstanding Community Service in Literature from AWP, the 2011 Barnes & Noble Writers for Writers Award from Poets & Writers, and the 2008 American Book Award for her book, *All That Lies Between Us*. She is the Founder/Executive Director of the Poetry Center at Passaic County Community College, editor of the *Paterson Literary Review*, and director of the creative writing program/professor of English at Binghamton University-SUNY. She has published 23 books, including *Paterson Light and Shadow* (Serving House Books, 2017), *What Blooms in Winter* (NYQ Books, 2016), and *Girls in the Chartreuse Jackets* (Cat in the Sun Books, 2014). Visit her website at www.mariagillan.com

Paul M. Levitt: If I ask myself how I turned out to be me, a retired English professor who writes the occasional scholarly article and historical novels, I return to the memory of time and remember a Russian father who told me folk tales, a mother who shared the events of her difficult life, a supportive sister, and a love of sports and reading. Brought up to believe that mercy eclipses justice, I believe that who can protest and does not is an accomplice.

Beverly Matherne's sixth bilingual work, *Bayou des Acadiens / Blind River*, short stories and prose poems, is from Éditions Perce-Neige.

She is one of eight authors, including Samuel Beckett, whose bilingual writing process is the subject of a completed doctoral dissertation from the University of Paris III. Widely published, she has received seven first-place prizes, including the Hackney Literary Award for Poetry, and is Professor Emerita of English at Northern Michigan University, where she served as director of the MFA program in creative writing.

Carol Menkiti, the wife of Ifeanyi A. Menkiti, the owner of the famous Grolier Poetry Book Shop in Cambridge, Massachusetts, is the Special Liaison at the bookshop.

Tino Villanueva writes and also paints. He's the author of seven books of poetry. His *Scene from the Movie GIANT* (1993) won a 1994 American Book Award. Six of his poems appear in *The Norton Anthology of Latino Literature* (2011). His art work appears on the covers/inside pages of: *Green Mountains Review, TriQuarterly, Parnassus*. Latest book of poems: *So Spoke Penelope* (2013), recently translated into Spanish and Italian as *Así habló Penélope* (2014), and *Così parlò Penelope*, respectively. He retired from Boston University, June 2015.

POEMS SUPPLEMENT

English Tea

In memory of Aeronwy Thomas Brynhart Ellis

In the very early morning
at Casa Barkan,
she was always up,
but so was I.

Coming down the Trapani-tiled stairwell,
she said, "Don't you ever sleep?
Did you put the kettle on?"

Yes, of course. It was always on,
with the box of tea at the ready.

It was time for English tea.
Only that kind of tea would do,
with a spot of milk, of course.

This was the tea that sustained
the Brits through the Blitz.

She was in her nightdress,
it was thin,
and she herself was
a bit transparent.

Frail, with curled hair,
the same curl that curled
her as Dylan's daughter
and her own daughter
in the froth of the Taf estuary,
still strong, like a sapling in the wind,
she had to bear the burden
of her father's rich legacy.

But, after so many years now,
of representing him
and finding her own poetic voice,
she bore the burden lightly on her
thin but very determined shoulders.

Yet no one knew,
as she would not say
(so private she was),
that the force that was inside her,
in her blood,
was sapping the life from her.

Always up and ready to go,
she drank her English tea,
and we were off
to the poetry races.

Beyond Swansea birthplace
and Laugharne boathouse,
and even Catania, Rome, the Abruzzi,
beyond Long Island–
Salem, Boston, Cambridge,
Michigan, Illinois, Iowa, Colorado–
all across America–
from New York to California and back.

I think it was English tea
that fueled and sustained her.

"Put the kettle on!"

Stanley H. Barkan

ACKNOWLEDGMENT:
First published in *Poetry Monthly International* (#20 June 2010),
United Kingdom, edited by Martin Holroyd.

Punta Los Lopos, Carmel Bay, California

Seals look like the dead
matter on a sandfloor
brought there in a burp
of a sealion wave.

We've battled through
stinging oak to get here
to hear the bark
of a seal

waking from slumber
ready to slip sleek
into a wave of foaming white
rhythmic, inevitable.

A cormorant dives for fish
emerges yards away
by islands of seaweed
the waters peacock blue.

Two seagulls perch
On seabound rock
chat amongst themselves
preen

letting the seals
seawolves
predate the fishy waters,
prowlers.

Coated and mufflered
I'm waiting here
on the cliff
away from the crumbly edge

crunching needles of
Monterey fir
stripped by the winds
to a petrified marker

the end of the world
the smell of yerba nueva
and wild lilac
in the undergrowth.

We've walked through
grey mauve blooms
on our way here
to the edge

of a seaworld
seals and birds
los lopos marinyas
gabbing gulls

I am looking and laughing
in the salt-laden air
as I loose my footing
and the cliff disappears.

Aeronwy Thomas

The Shade

A chubby man
followed me
to the library
along the streets
of Boston
past Dunkin' Donuts
And Peets coffee and teas
into the pharmacy
for Vick's Vaporub
hence
to Harvard
and leafy trees.
His shadow
followed me
up the steps
through the doors
of the public halls.
The throng already there
greeted the shadow
and not me
with loud applause
in the dusty halls
until he faded from sight
to his proper shape
a shade
and I stepped forward
flesh and blood
to shout to the wind
the stars and the rain
to be acclaimed
by the crowd
in my own right
for a while free

of the shame
not to be him again
free
of the shadow
that keeps pace with me
throughout my life
that dogs my steps.

Aeronwy Thomas

Carl Sandburg's Birthplace, Illinois
(for Robin and Liz)

1.

We enter your birthplace,
no bigger than a shed
on a rich person's lawn.

It's furnished to suggest
a true sense of your home,
wooden, simple, Mid-West poor.

In the museum room,
we observe your guitar
that would give out fresh sounds

to family and friends.
In the garden the stone
where the dust of you rests,

and the paving-slab path
that's marked with quotations,
the fine lines from your poems.

2.

In Galesburg, Carl Sandburg,
I feel your warm spirit,
a quick whiff of your life,

a loud freight train cutting
the town in half, a mad
downpour of a dark storm

coming; and then, later,
the breathless, flattened breadth
of the open landscape;

fields yawning to an edge
it seems no-one will reach,
a sprawling stretch of wheat,

the occasional barn,
trees, pylons, and a sky
that's as big as heaven.

Peter Thabit Jones

Harvard University, Boston

In the library
at Harvard,

we listen to tapes
of your father,

his stage voice
loud in the headphones.

Then, after coffee,
we are shown some photos,

rare and precious,
of him off-guard,

laughing, the famous face
friendly, mischievous.

Dylan Thomas
being Dylan.

In Chicago,
you show me a poem

in the making,
a page of your thoughts,

rough lines and shaped notes
finding their rhythm,

a daughter's quick scribbling
towards some shade of truth.

Peter Thabit Jones

Sometimes
(for Aeronwy)

Sometimes when sipping
a tea inside Starbucks
in Merrick, New York,
or searching a drugstore
for vitamins in Illinois,
or running late
to a terminal gate,
your face *really* looked
like your father's
in that painting
by Augustus John.
The young Dylan,
boy-faced, too pretty,
that I bought
as a poster
when almost sixteen.

Peter Thabit Jones

BIO OF STANLEY H. BARKAN

Stanley H. Barkan.
© 2018 Bill Wolak

Stanley H. Barkan, born 1936, in Brooklyn, is a retired teacher, poet, translator, editor, presenter, and small press publisher. He grew up in East New York among many who fled Nazi-dominated Europe. He was fascinated by the languages they spoke and the stories they told of how and why they left Europe. This interest in other languages and the cultures in which they are embedded formed the basis of his life and work as a cross-culturalist, avidly seeking to learn and explore different languages and cultures. He draws his inspiration from the place he came from (Brooklyn), the many friends he's known along the way, the extraordinary creative people he's met and worked with in his world travels–their languages and cultures, their poetry, stories, songs, music, and dramas–his pet cats, and, most of all, his family–forebears, children, and, his grandchildren.

As a publisher, he has, to date, published some 450 editions in 59 languages (including such notables as Isaac Asimov, Stanley Kunitz,

Gregory Rabassa, I. B. Singer), more than 500 broadsides (most notably, *Sicilian Antigruppo,* illustrated by Bebe Barkan; *The Artist / L'Artiste,* lithographs by Tchouki; and *Cross-Cultural Communications Bilingual Broadsides,* with photoart by Adel Gorgy), and postcards (*To Struga with Love,* portfolio, and a series of boxed editions, including: *Cat Poems, Love Poems, Women Poems, Cajun Poems, Mother Poems*).

As a poet, his own work has been translated into more than 25 languages, ranging from Arabic to Yiddish. Bilingual editions of his poetry include: Bulgarian (*Naming the Birds,* translated by Vladimir Levchev), Chinese (*Sailing the Yangtze,* translated by Hong Ai Bai; *No Cats on the Yangtze* and *Gambling in Macáu,* translated by Zhao Si), Italian (*Bubbemeise & Babbaluci,* translated by Nina & Nat Scammacca); Polish (*Under the Apple Tree / Pod jablonia,* translated by Adam Szyper, and *Wiersze Wybrane,* translated by Tomasz Marek Sobieraj), Romanian (*The Machine for Inventing Ideals / Ma ina de Inventat Idealuri* and *Seasons/Anotimpuri caudate,* translated by Olimpia Iacob), Russian (*Crossings,* translated by Aleksey Dayen w/Victoria Markova), Sicilian (*The Machine for Inventing Ideals / Ma ina de Inventat Idealuri* and *Seasons/Anotimpuri caudate,* translated by Marc Scalabrino), and Spanish (*As Still as a Broom / Tan quieto como una escoba,* translated by Isaac Goldemberg).

The many awards he has received include: In 1991, Poets House and the NYC Board of Education presented him with the Poetry Teacher of the Year Award. In 1996, he received the Poor Richard's Award, "for a quarter century of high quality publishing" from the Small Press Center in New York. In 2011, in celebration of CCC's 40th Anniversary, Barkan received four plaque awards: one from The Faculty of the Creative Arts Department at Siena College, New York, "In Sincere Appreciation of 40 Years of Success in the Art of Publishing"; a second from the Korean Expatriate Literature Association, Los Angeles "for his contribution to the promotion of the globalization of Korean literature through exchanges of Korean and American poetry"; a third from The Seventh Biennial Warren County Poetry Festival "in recognition of 40 years as Publisher & Editor of Cross-Cultural Communications and world-wide promotion of poets"; and a fourth from The Poetry Center at Passaic County Community College "The Paterson Literary Review Award (PLR) for Lifetime Service to Literature." In 2014, he also received the Korean Expatriate Literature's plaque for "the promotion of the globalization of Korean Literature" and the international bilingual Bengali poetry magazine, *Shabdaguchha*'s "Lifetime Achievement Award (both 2013); and the special commemorative "Stanley H. Barkan" issue of *The Seventh Quarry* with a plaque "for over 40 years of literary excellence." Most recent awards include the following: 2016 [Trapani, Sicily] – L'Occhio di Scammacca (sculpture) Sicilian award; in 2016, The Homer European Medal of Poetry and Art; in China: Best Poet of the Year 8 January 2017, The International Poetry Translation and Research Centre, *The Journal of The World Poets Quarterly* (Multilingual), 2018 Poetry Prize (medal) of European Academy of Sciences Arts and Literature (January 26, 2018, in Paris).

He's looking forward to compiling his *On the Milkboxes: New & Selected Poems*, his memoir *Tales of a Cross-Culturalist: The Saga of a Small Press Publisher*, and completing the preparation of his CCC archives for a university that considers itself to be "a mini-Library of Congress." In the past, he has directed cultural programs at the International Center in New York, the Small Press Center, many of the Small Press Book Fair poetry programs, programs at Poets House, the International Writing Series at both the Barnes & Noble flagship store in Manhattan and the Borders superstore on Long Island, and the International Poetry Series at the UN's Dag Hammarskjöld Center, as well as programs in Puerto Rico, Sicily, and Wales. Currently, he coordinates the new Yale Club Poetry Series in Manhattan.

Barkan lives with his artist-wife, Bebe, in Merrick, Long Island. Their married children and spouses with their children–Mia & Steven and Natasha & Roxy; Scotte & Jackie and Mattingly & Jeremy & Justin–live nearby in the same town.

BIO OF AERONWY THOMAS

Aeronwy Thomas.
© 2008 Peter Thabit Jones

Aeronwy Thomas (Aeronwy Bryn Thomas-Ellis, 3rd March 1943– 27th July 2009), the daughter of Dylan and Caitlin Thomas, was born in London and predominantly brought up in Laugharne, West Wales. She achieved a B.A. Hons in English and Comparative Religion at Isleworth College, a TEFL Diploma at Working Adult Education College and was awarded an Honorary Fellowship from the University of Wales, Swansea in 2003 and from the Swansea Institute (now the Swansea Metropolitan University) in 2004. She worked in London as a trainee nurse, a publicist for Dino de Laurentiis film studio, and as a journalist in Rome and elsewhere. She was a writer, poet and performer and taught creative writing and Italian in Adult Education.

Apart from her books of poetry, she wrote many articles for numerous magazines and newspapers. Poems have appeared in various magazines and anthologies in the UK and in America. She gave talks and interviews worldwide, performed at many festivals and other events and appeared in many documentaries on the arts and poetry, notably The Southbank Show, The English Programme (CH4), Arena, the BBC's *Do not go gentle*, and *Dylan on Dylan: To Begin at the Beginning*, a film directed by Andrew Sinclair (the director of the film version of *Under Milk Wood*), and most acted as a research consultant for the film, *The Edge of Love*, starring Sienna Miller, Keira Knightley, Matthew Rhys, and Cillian Murphy.

She was closely associated with the Dylan Thomas Society and was instrumental in having a plaque for her father placed in Poets' Corner, Westminster Abbey. Aeronwy, who died on 27 July 2009, lived in South West London with her husband, Trefor, a tenor with the London Welsh Chorale. They have two children: a son, Huw, and a daughter, Hannah. *My Father's Places*, her portrait of her childhood with her famous father and mother, was published posthumously with much acclaim from critics and readers.

ABOUT THE AUTHOR

Portrait of Peter Thabit Jones.
© 2018 Svetlana Deric Jannace

Peter Thabit Jones was born in Wales and raised by his maternal grandparents. He is the author of fourteen books, several of which have been reprinted and four published in Romania. His work has been translated into over twenty languages.

In March 2008 Peter's American publisher, Stanley H. Barkan, organised a six week poetry reading tour for Peter and Dylan Thomas's daughter, Aeronwy. The pair gave readings and workshops from New York to California, at many universities and prestigious art venues. Peter is also the co-author, with Aeronwy, of the *Dylan Thomas Walking Tour of Greenwich Village*.

He was invited to Serbia in 2006 by the Serbian Writers' Association to participate in the 43rd International Meeting of Writers in Belgrade. He was visiting poet in Romania in 2008 and 2009, where he carried out readings and poetry workshops at colleges and universities.

He resided at Big Sur, California, in the summer of 2010 as writer-in-residence, returning again for summer residencies each year from 2011 to 2018.

Whilst in California in 2012, Peter wrote his drama *The Fire in the Wood*, about Big Sur sculptor Edmund Kara, who is famous for his sculpture of Elizabeth Taylor in the film *The Sandpiper*.

Peter has participated in many festivals and conferences in America and Europe, including World Affairs Conference, Colorado, 2009; NEMLA Conferences, (Boston, 2013, Pennsylvania, 2014, and Toronto, 2015); and the Massachusetts Poetry Festival. He has also organised A Visiting American Students/Dylan Thomas in Wales Project with Knox College, America, 2010, and an International Poetry Festival, 2011, and a Drama Festival, 2012, at the Dylan Thomas Theatre, Swansea. The latter two events were part of an ongoing collaboration with Cross-Cultural Communications, New York.

In 2014, he was a participant in a number of DT100 events in the UK and in America celebrating the Centenary of the birth of Dylan Thomas. The *Dylan Thomas Walking Tour of Greenwich Village, New York* book and smartphone app were both launched, the app by the Right Honourable Carwyn Jones, the First Minister of Wales, accompanied by Peter and Hannah Ellis, Dylan's granddaughter, in New York. Peter was also the co-organiser of a Dylan Thomas Multilingual/International Creative Writing Competition and the organiser of a Dylan Thomas Centenary Quotations Trail at the National Waterfront Museum, Swansea.

His short drama, *The Poet, the Hunchback, and The Boy,* based on the poem 'The hunchback in the park' by Dylan Thomas, is available as a DVD. It was part of the Centenary celebrations of the Dylan Thomas Theatre, Swansea. The drama was performed by Theatre actors at the National Waterfront Museum in Swansea and at The Welsh Centre in London, in May 2013.

Peter is the Founder and Editor of *The Seventh Quarry Swansea Poetry Magazine*, which publishes poetry, translations, interviews, and articles from around the world, and the accompanying The Seventh Quarry Press, which publishes international books of poetry, prose, and art.

His poem *Kilvey Hill* has been incorporated into a permanent stained-glass window at Saint Thomas Community School in Swansea. In April 2014, he was inducted into the Phi Sigma Iota Society at Salem State University, Massachusetts, for his contribution to literature and literary translations.

He is the recipient of the Eric Gregory Award for Poetry (The Society of Authors, London), The Society of Authors Award, The Royal Literary Fund Award (London) and an Arts Council of Wales Award. He has been a prizewinner in several UK and international poetry competitions. He was awarded the Ted Slade Award for Service to Poetry in 2016 by The Poetry Kit (UK), the Shabdaguchha Poetry Award 2017 (USA), and the 2017 Homer: European Medal for Art and Poetry.

His poem *Lament for Soldiers of the First World War* is featured in the film *Bells on the Western Front*, produced by Holly Tree Productions. The film has won several international awards including First Prize in the 2017 Wales International Film Festival.

His chamber opera libretto, *Ermesinde's Long Walk*, for composer Albena Petrovic, premiered at the Philarmonie Luxembourg in 2017 and his full orchestra libretto for her with Svetla Georgieva, *Love and Jealousy*, premiered at the National Opera House Stara Zagora in Bulgaria in May 2018. *Ermesinde's Long Walk* also premiered at National Opera House Stara Zagora in December 2018.

His drama, *The Fire in the Wood*, about Californian sculptor Edmund Kara, premiered at the Actors Studio of Newburyport in Massachusetts in April 2017 and at the Henry Miller Library and the Carl Cherry Center in California in May/June 2018. His verse drama, *The Boy and the Lion's Head*, was performed at the Swansea International Festival of Music and the Arts in 2018.

Further information: www.peterthabitjones.com